THE
Uncertain
TRUMPET

Maxwell D. Taylor
General, U.S. Army (Retired)
CHIEF OF STAFF, 1955-1959

☆ THE
☆ *Uncertain*
☆ TRUMPET
☆

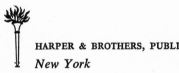

HARPER & BROTHERS, PUBLISHERS
New York

CONTENTS

FOREWORD ix

I The Great Fallacy 1

II The Rise of the Doctrine of Massive Retaliation 11

III The New Look in Action, 1953-1956 23

IV The New Look Ages, 1956-1959 47

V The Making of Our Military Strategy— Theory 80

VI The Joint Chiefs of Staff at Work 88

VII The Failure of Decision-Making: How Military Strategy Is Formulated in Fact 115

VIII Flexible Response—A New National Military Program 130

IX A New and Certain Trumpet 165

APPENDIX 181

INDEX 199

For if the trumpet give an uncertain sound, who shall prepare himself to the battle?

I CORINTHIANS 14:8

FOREWORD

DURING the weeks preceding D-Day in Normandy, June 6, 1944, those of us in command of the American airborne assault were deeply concerned over new activities of the Germans in the parachute- and glider-landing areas which we planned to use in Normandy. Day after day the air photographs of the zone showed new defensive works apparently to resist an airborne attack. The photo interpreters told us that they consisted mainly of poles some eight inches in diameter and eight feet in height which were being planted in dense checkerboard patterns across many of the Norman fields. It occurred to us at once that if we studied the pattern of this poling activity, we might determine the German plan of defense. At least we would know how they expected us to land.

Night after night we pored over the new photographs at my division headquarters at Newbury in Berkshire, England. But try as we would, we were unable to find any meaningful pattern in these German efforts. The poles sprang up everywhere but there was no evidence of plan in the choice of site or of priority to complete the work in one area ahead of any other. Thus, we took off at dusk on June 5, still puzzled as to German intentions and dispositions.

Landing with my stick of parachutists in the darkness of D-Day morning, I assembled a handful of our troops and surrounded the first farmhouse which we found. After getting information about the Germans in the vicinity, I asked the farmer about the poling of his fields.

"I see you have poles in this small field to the west of your house, but none in that big one to the east. Why is that?"

"Oh," said the farmer, "the Germans told us to pole all of our fields by June 15. My cow never liked that west field, so I poled it first."

That was it. In this particular case, at least, there was no more rational basis for the German defensive plan than the preference of this Frenchman's cow. I suspect that a similar lack of plan had prevailed throughout the Norman countryside. While the story has its humorous side, it is a reminder of what happens when military plans and actions are controlled by other than military factors. The poles placed to the whims of the French cows had no real effect on our landing.

I have undertaken to write this book because of my conviction that the defense of the United States is presently controlled largely by nonmilitary factors or by military factors which have become outmoded. While there are strong arguments for a cooling period after leaving the post of Chief of Staff before committing my views to writing, I have the deep feeling that there is no time to wait. We are faced with declining military strength at a time of increasing political tension. To arrest this trend before it goes too far requires certain immediate actions to be taken—the "quick fixes" described herein. The permanent remedy calls for a complete reappraisal of our strategy by the responsible agencies of our government. If this book can suggest one possible way to solve the problem and thereby get this vital reappraisal under way, it will have served its purpose.

In setting forth the problem, I have found it necessary to talk at some length about the defense budget. This may appear a drab subject but, if it performs its proper function, the budget is far more than a compilation of dusty figures of interest only to fiscal experts. It should be a translation into dollars of the military strategy upon which our future security will depend. Since the funds it provides will influence the military programs three to four years into the future, the budget in effect mortgages the freedom of decision and action of our leaders over a similarly long period. Hence, if we are to change our ways of doing our defense business, it should be done now before another annual budget projects past mistakes even farther into the future. If our trumpet is to give a changed sound, now is the time to retune it.

My former colleagues at the Pentagon will find little new in this book. I have voiced most of these views and criticisms repeatedly within the Department of Defense during my four years as Chief of Staff. In general, for fear of inaccurate quotation, I have not tried to record in detail the counterarguments of the competent and patriotic men among my associates who have disagreed with me. Needless to say, their views are worthy of the most serious consideration before taking any of the actions I recommend herein. A final solution to our strategic needs should be a co-operative effort of the best minds of all the military services.

There may be spots in the text where the reader feels the need of more information about what took place. I have been obliged to write with a careful eye to the requirements of security and propriety. These considerations have resulted in some omissions, but I do not believe they are important to the theme.

While the responsibility for this book is my own, I have obviously been helped directly or indirectly by many able men and women. I have had the benefit of association with an understanding and courageous Secretary of the Army, Wilbur M. Brucker. He has set an example to all of us in uniform of a civilian leader willing to take responsibility and to fight stanchly for any cause in which he believed. Many officers of the Army staff have influenced my views with regard to many of the important issues discussed in this book. They have been keen and discerning critics of the logic with which I have pleaded my case before the Joint Chiefs of Staff and elsewhere. Insofar as I have allowed them, they have fulfilled the role of the perfect staff officer who sees to it that the Old Man's mistakes are neither too big nor too numerous. My inspiring association with these able men has been one of the great rewards of the position of Chief of Staff.

Thus, it is impossible to acknowledge the contribution of the many individuals to whom I am indebted for some form of assistance in writing this book. However, I cannot fail to mention my senior aide, Lieutenant Colonel Bernard W. Rogers, Warrant Officer John J. Proctor and Specialist Johnnie L. Scott, all of my immediate office. The members of my family, particularly my wife, Lydia, and my son and daughter-in-law, John and Priscilla Taylor, have been most helpful in representing and defending the nonprofessional, civilian point of view. Mr. Evan Thomas of Harper has assisted in that particularly difficult task of reducing, if not eliminating, the technical language and the stuffiness of the Pentagon which inevitably cling to the pen of a long-time denizen.

I was asked recently what in my past experience had been most helpful to me as Chief of Staff. Was it attendance at the Command and Staff College and the Army War College? Was it service alongside General Marshall at the time of Pearl Harbor? Was it command of the 101st Airborne Division in Europe in World War II or of the Eighth Army in Korea? I never hesitated in replying, "My most valuable preparation was membership in the Northeast High School Society of Debate in my pre-West Point days in Kansas City." The subsequent chapters will show the reader why.

MAXWELL D. TAYLOR

THE
Uncertain
TRUMPET

CHAPTER I

THE GREAT FALLACY

THE WAR diary which I kept as Commanding General of the 101st Airborne Division in World War II carries the following entry: "28 July 1945 (Saturday). Drove to Berchtesgaden for luncheon with General Marshall and General Patton. Attended II Corps track meet and returned with General Marshall to Berchtesgadener Hof. Heard for the first time about A-Bomb."

Here is the background of this entry. V-E Day had found the 101st Airborne Division racing across southern Bavaria with Berchtesgaden as its objective. This famous resort of Hitler remained with Berlin the last uncaptured symbols of Nazism. Although this rugged mountainous area was reportedly to be a national redoubt, organized and defended for a fight to the finish, actually it fell easily to the combined efforts of the 3rd U.S. Infantry Division, the 2nd French Armored Division, and the 101st Airborne Division. The last hostile shots which I saw fired in World War II came from a German machine gun in a mountain pass just to the west of Berchtesgaden.

Once installed in this scenic spot at the foot of the Alps,

the division began to receive many notable visitors. Some came in great haste—they were German leaders fleeing from capture by the advancing Russian forces to the east. Field Marshal Kesselring, the German Commander in Italy, General Guderian, the great Panzer leader, and many lesser lights turned themselves over to our airborne troops. Others of our callers came more leisurely—they were U.S. leaders or those of our Allies.

Under such conditions it was a great joy to me to receive word in late July, 1945, that General Marshall, with whom I had served closely on the War Department General Staff at the outset of the war, was coming from the Potsdam Conference to pay us a visit. He sent word that he wished to rest quietly in Berchtesgaden but would like to have luncheon with General Patton, whose Third Army Headquarters was at Bad Tölz some seventy miles to the west.

I relayed General Marshall's desires to General Patton and at the appointed time went out to the Salzburg airstrip to meet the Chief of Staff. Upon his arrival, I took him to the Berchtesgadener Hof and installed him in an apartment which had often housed Nazi bigwigs in the past. General Patton arrived shortly before noon and the three of us lunched quietly in General Marshall's suite. After the lunch, where the conversation turned principally upon the events of the Potsdam Conference, I took my two distinguished guests out to the local sports field, where the athletes of the II Corps and of my division were having a track meet. The three of us sat in the warm Bavarian sunshine, somewhat apart from the other spectators. During a lull, General Marshall turned to General Patton and me and said quietly, "Gentlemen, I am going to tell you something of the utmost importance. When you hear what I have to say, there will be no need to caution you as to the need for silence."

Then General Marshall proceeded to tell us a story about which we had heretofore known nothing—the story of the explosion of the first atomic weapon at Alamogordo, New Mexico, on July 16, just twelve days before. He described briefly the development of the Manhattan District under the leadership of Major General Leslie R. Groves, Jr., the great difficulties which Groves and his colleagues had overcome and the final triumph of the successful detonation. He explained jokingly—and I think it was to add to our obvious bewilderment—that this was not an "explosion" but an "implosion."

After describing the terrific yield of the detonation and some of its obvious military implications, General Marshall closed the discussion by saying—and I shall never forget the words—"Gentlemen, on the first moonlight night in August, we will drop one of these bombs on the Japanese. I don't think we will need more than two."

General Patton and I looked at each other in silence, both meditating upon the awful significance of Marshall's words. I, at least, was trying to imagine what the effect of these weapons might be on the war in the Pacific and from there passed readily to a conjecture as to the possible mean-

3

ing of these weapons in future warfare. What if we had had such things to clear our way across Europe? Think of the thousands of our brave soldiers whose lives might have been spared. Now, indeed, I thought, we have a weapon which can keep the peace and never again will a Hitler or a Mussolini dare to use war to impose his will upon the Free World.

Such were my thoughts, at least; what General Patton thought I shall never know, as this was the last time that I saw him alive. But it is safe to say that we were both sensing the fascination of the Great Fallacy, that henceforth the use or the threatened use of atomic weapons of mass destruction would be sufficient to assure the security of the United States and its friends. To show that this concept is indeed a fallacy is a primary purpose of this book.

History was soon to prove that General Marshall's estimate of the effect of the new atomic weapon on Japan was correct. Two bombs did do the job. The Japanese surrendered, the victory was won, and the nuclear age had dawned. Even more than the generals at the Berchtesgaden track meet, the whole world was deeply impressed with the awesome power of the new weapons in the hands of the United States. Our own people were quick to believe that our armed forces had in the air-delivered atomic bomb the absolute weapon which would permit the United States, its sole possessor, to police the world through the threat of its use. Thus, in 1945 a new strategic creed, eventually to be known as Massive Retaliation, came into being, and later reached full acceptance as military orthodoxy in the so-called New Look program adopted by our government in 1953. Along the way it received a setback from the events of the Korean War, which contradicted many of its basic assumptions. But it survived and continued to thrive even under the vicissitudes which are recorded in this book. In spite of temporary reverses, Massive Retaliation remains the basic strategic concept which guides our military preparations today. While occasional statements of spokesmen for national defense sometimes seem to contradict unqualified faith in Massive Retaliation, the real strength of that faith is shown in the figures of the annual military defense budget. Here, since the end of the Korean War and in spite of its lessons, the dollars have always gone to support in top priority the requirements of Massive Retaliation and of general atomic war. "Where your treasure is, there will your heart be also."

It is my belief that Massive Retaliation as a guiding strategic concept has reached a dead end and that there is an urgent need for a reappraisal of our strategic needs. In its heyday, Massive Retaliation could offer our leaders only two choices, the initiation of general nuclear war or compromise and retreat. From its earliest days, many world events have occurred which cast doubt on its validity and exposed its fallacious character. Korea, a limited conventional war, fought by the United States when we had an atomic monopoly, was clear disproof of its universal efficacy. The many other limited wars which have occurred since

1945—the Chinese civil war, the guerrilla warfare in Greece and Malaya, Vietnam, Taiwan, Hungary, the Middle East, Laos, to mention only a few—are clear evidence that, while our massive retaliatory strategy may have prevented the Great War—a World War III—it has not maintained the Little Peace; that is, peace from disturbances which are little only in comparison with the disaster of general war.

Other developments also call for a reappraisal of our military strategy. We have lost our former atomic monopoly. We are probably inferior to the USSR in numbers of ballistic missiles. We have no antiballistic missiles as a defense to offset this superiority in offense. We have made no realistic effort to cope with Communist strength on the ground. Anemia is afflicting many of our military alliances. We are playing a losing game and should change it. But this change is made difficult by the weaknesses of our strategy-making machinery and procedures. In particular, the Joint Chiefs of Staff system has proved ineffective and needs a fundamental overhaul as a preliminary to a general reappraisal of our strategy.

The strategic doctrine which I would propose to replace Massive Retaliation is called herein the Strategy of Flexible Response. This name suggests the need for a capability to react across the entire spectrum of possible challenge, for coping with anything from general atomic war to infiltrations and aggressions such as threaten Laos and Berlin in 1959. The new strategy would recognize that it is just as necessary to deter or win quickly a limited war as to deter general war. Otherwise, the limited war which we cannot win quickly may result in our piecemeal attrition or involvement in an expanding conflict which may grow into the general war we all want to avoid.

To make this change in strategy will require a lot of doing. It will call first for a clear directive from the National Security Council to the Department of Defense. It will require night work by the Joint Chiefs of Staff to translate the directive into priorities of military requirements. It will need a new kind of defense budget to see that the dollars follow the approved priorities. These actions in combination would comprise the Military Program of Flexible Response which is urgently needed to overcome the serious military disadvantages which we face vis-à-vis the Soviets in the period 1961-1964.

Any serious discussion of the problems of national security requires at the outset an agreement as to the meaning of certain basic terms. Already the expressions "general" and "limited" war call for definition. I shall use them in the early part of this book as presently defined in the strategy-making circles of the government. It should be clear, however, that I do not agree with these definitions, as my subsequent comments will indicate. But, for the present purposes, the term "general war" will designate a conflict in which the forces of the United States and the USSR are directly involved and in which atomic weapons are assumed to be used from the outset. On the other hand, "limited war" will be considered to be a conflict short of

7

general war in which the United States forces will use atomic weapons as required to achieve national objectives. The proponents of these definitions hold that these local conflicts are likely to occur in the less-developed areas of the world outside of Europe and that only limited U.S. forces will be necessary to cope with them.

These definitions have achieved currency in official circles only after very sharp debate and continued efforts are being made to change them. The objection to the "general war" definition is that it appears to require that in any case where U.S. and Soviet forces come into contact, regardless of the dimensions or the political importance of the incident, we would initiate all-out atomic bombing as the proper response. This matter of definitions is not an academic point; it can have very practical effects. For example, insistence upon this definition can stultify sensible planning for a situation such as might arise if the USSR or its allies blocked our access to Berlin. In planning for such a contingency, the definitions can be used as an argument against using U.S. ground forces as a probe to determine Soviet intentions and thus to avoid the possibility of our being kept out of Berlin by a bluff. Since such an action might bring U.S. troops into armed conflict with Russians, it could lead to general war—if indeed we are serious about this definition of general war. Common sense will say that we are not but, as it is still in the official lexicon of the strategic planners, I will adhere to the definition except when otherwise noted.

The "limited war" definition is defective because it seems

to exclude the possibility of any limited war in the NATO area of Western Europe. This argument is always cropping up in Pentagon debate, even though one limited war in the NATO area has occurred, namely the Greek Civil War in 1947, to which the U.S. made a significant contribution in military advisers and military equipment. Even though the U.S. possessed an atomic monopoly at the time, no one proposed to use atomic weapons and to expand the localized hostilities into general war. The connotation of intrinsic smallness in the definition of limited wars is objectionable because it can be used to keep the armed services from planning for limited situations much greater than the landing in Lebanon in 1958. It has even led its extreme partisans to deny that the Korean conflict qualified as a limited war, despite its obvious limitations as to geography, weapons, and political objectives.

Both definitions encourage the armed forces to a dependence upon the use of atomic weapons to a degree which is open to question. In general war, atomic weapons would be used at once; in limited war, in accord with the national interest. While there has been no occasion to test the validity of this assumption in general war, it is significant that during the Lebanon landing in 1958, the United States Army had an Honest John rocket afloat off Beirut but was not allowed to land it because it could fire an atomic warhead as well as a conventional one. In this instance, our political leaders felt that it was against the national interest even to suggest by the presence of the weapon that we might use atomic weapons in Lebanon. Additionally, the sudden destructiveness of general war and the relative insignificance of limited war, as portrayed by the definitions, are used as arguments against maintaining reserves of trained manpower and military equipment to support extended military operations. Thus, it may be fairly said that these definitions set the configuration of our military strategy. They are used to justify a strategy of Massive Retaliation and to rule out a consideration of the needs of nonnuclear war without first being themselves justified. To explain their existence requires a review of the evolution of the strategy of Massive Retaliation and the causes of the thinking behind it.

CHAPTER II

THE RISE OF THE DOCTRINE
OF MASSIVE RETALIATION

THE DOCTRINE which under the name of Massive Retaliation eventually became the central theme of the military strategy of the United States has its origin in the theories of the Italian General Giulio Douhet prior to World War II and the influence of these theories on the thinking of the United States Air Force. General Douhet thought, and generations of Air Force officers were taught to believe, that strategic bombing of an enemy's industrial and urban centers could win a war. In World War II the U.S. Air Force as well as the Royal Air Force of Great Britain undertook to implement this doctrine. They were encouraged to massive bombing of urban targets by the early example of the attacks of the Luftwaffe on the cities of Great Britain and other Allied countries. As control of the air passed to the side of the Allies in the course of the war, they were able to make massive air attacks on German cities against little opposition. While these attacks devastated most of the urban areas of Germany, they were surprisingly ineffective in reducing the German industrial output in support of the war effort. Following World War II, an analysis was made of the effectiveness of this bombing and the results compiled in the *U.S. Strategic Bombing Survey*. Herein it was conclusively shown that strategic bombing in World War II had not been decisive in destroying the war production of Nazi Germany. It was a contributing but not the decisive factor in achieving the ultimate victory. Thus, the partisans of General Douhet could find but limited support for their claims in the results of the war in Europe.

The war in Japan ended on a different note. The atomic explosions over Hiroshima and Nagasaki provided a new case for the decisive character of strategic bombing. The atomic bomb offered air power a new weapon with tremendously increased destructiveness and encouraged once more the belief that an ultimate weapon was in the hands of our Air Force which would allow the United States to impose a sort of Pax Americana on the world. The corollary to this belief was that conventional military forces would have little or no value in the new era.

Nuclear weapons began to exert an important influence on military policy immediately following World War II, although their capabilities, limitations, and political implications were only vaguely understood. But it seemed clear that they represented destructiveness at a cheap price. This point was important because of the need to replace the armed forces demobilized so thoroughly and wastefully at the end of World War II in the furor to "bring the boys home." To have rebuilt similar forces in the succeeding years would have been costly both in dollars and in political "face."

Neither the Truman Administration nor the American people were prepared to foot such a bill, particularly that part of the program which would have been a tacit admission of lack of foresight. Under such circumstances, it is not surprising that the idea of relying on nuclear weapons and strategic bombing for national defense had great appeal. Such a military program appeared to offer us a way out of fighting dirty, costly wars with Communist masses on the ground. It was a way to meet manpower with mechanical power. Its apparent cheapness gave rise to the slogan, "More bang for a buck." But this reliance on Massive Retaliation overlooked the fact that atomic bangs could eventually be bought for rubles as well as dollars.

In such a postwar climate, it was probably natural for the U.S. to do most of its defense spending for air power and atomic weapon systems. It is true that current events, such as the Communist-led civil war in Greece, the Communist coup in Czechoslovakia and the Russian blockade of Berlin, should have been reminders of the need to meet challenges to which the atomic bomb would be no reply. However, the lesson, if perceived, was not effective and conventional forces were sacrificed to the needs of atomic power.

Expenditures for the Army decreased steadily during Fiscal Years 1948, 1949, and 1950, while Air Force expenditures showed a sharp upward turn. Army strength dropped from eighty-nine divisions in 1945 to ten divisions in Fiscal Year 1950. The Navy and Air Force also lost conventional strength during this period, but not so much. In spite of a bitter public controversy with the Navy, the Air Force was allowed to proceed with the dubious B-36 program as a part of the expansion of long-range, nuclear strike forces.

In July, 1950, the North Koreans crossed the 38th Parallel, U.S. forces were thrown into battle and the war was on. The direct involvement of United States forces in this remote and relatively unknown country and the character of the subsequent military operations provided a rough jolt to the proponents of Massive Retaliation. If the dogma were right, the threat or the use of airborne atomic weapons in Korea and North China should have been sufficient to win a quick victory. But the fact was that, for reasons sufficient unto our responsible leaders at the time, the United States preferred to fight a limited war for limited objectives without the use of atomic weapons, even though our country had an absolute monopoly of these weapons at the time. This was, and still is, a hard fact for many military polemists to swallow. They can only belabor the folly of having accepted the conflict on such restricted terms. This, they say, was fighting a war with one arm tied behind our back. Had our air power been released from the shackles imposed upon it, it could have carried the war to a successful conclusion by the unrestricted bombing of the sources of the hostile military power. Be that as it may, the responsible military and civilian leaders of the government considered all these arguments at the time and, rightly or wrongly, rejected them. As a result, the decisive action in thwarting the Communist aggression was ground action conducted very much as had been the operations of World War II. In spite of the overwhelming superiority of the United Nations in the air and on the sea, it was the infantry deployed along the rugged Korean hilltops which determined the issue of victory or defeat. The fluctuations of this front line on the ground provided the measure of success in the war.

As Eighth Army Commander in Korea I was deeply impressed with these facts and shortly after the Armistice wrote to General Ridgway the following observations:

An outstanding impression from the operations in Korea has been the ineffectiveness or inapplicability of many of our modern weapons to the requirement of the Korean type of limited war. I refer particularly to the weapons of the Air Force, the Navy and the Armor, to which certain other Army weapons and equipment may be added. The enemy, terrain, and weather combined to nullify in a large measure much of the costly equipment assembled during and after World War II in preparation for a possible World War III, to be fought principally in Western Europe. To these restrictions we added the subjective factor of our own reluctance to use atomic and other special weapons in which we have been investing a large part of the military budget.

The absence of an opponent prevented the useful employ-

ment of much of our air and naval strength. Except for the
MIG's in the northwest corner of the peninsula, there was no
airborne enemy to combat. Similarly, at sea the mightiest war
ships of the world were obliged to occupy themselves with
shelling relatively unimportant targets ashore, or with maintaining a blockade against negligible enemy naval forces.

Finally, we denied ourselves the use of special weapons [i.e.,
atomic weapons] for a variety of reasons, some military, some
political. A partial list of these deterrent causes include: reluctance to expend the surprise effect of these weapons on a
secondary enemy; doubt as to their effectiveness in the terrain
of Korea; fear of reprisals by enemy against Korean and
Japanese targets; resistance of our allies to any action which
might extend the war. Regardless of the merits of the case for
and against the use of special weapons in Korea, the fact that
we deliberately abstained from using them is a reminder that
we may do so again in future situations, particularly as the
Soviet atomic capability increases. In the end, by a tacitly
agreed, mutual cancelling out of special weapons, we may be
forced to rely again on conventional means.

Yet in the U.S., the ultimate effect of the Korean experience, oddly enough, was not to weaken faith in atomic
air power but rather to strengthen it. By the time of the
Armistice in 1953, the entire country had become heartily
sick of the Korean conflict and impatient at the frustra-
tions which it entailed. This popular dissatisfaction over
the indecisive nature of the conflict became an important
political factor in the presidential election of 1952. General

Eisenhower was elected on a platform which promised an early end to the repugnant stalemate allegedly the result of the mistakes of the Truman Administration.

No sooner was President Eisenhower in office than the new Administration proclaimed the New Look as the guiding military policy of the new government. In its principal aspects, the New Look was little more than the old air power dogma set forth in Madison Avenue trappings and now formally buttressed upon Massive Retaliation as the central strategic concept. Its ready acceptance had complex and varied causes, some of which have already been mentioned. They included such things as the domestic reaction to the Korean conflict, the continued faith in the efficacy of air power, a desire for budgetary economy, and the American penchant for simple solutions. Massive Retaliation and its attendant concept of a short, violent war were consistent with all of these points. Its implementation assumed the preponderant use of air power and avoidance of the bloody, exhausting battle on the ground. The postulated shortness of the conflict encouraged the hope of savings in the costs of a conventional mobilization, while the spectacular violence of Massive Retaliation appealed to our American frontier impulse to blast the villain who presumes to oppose us.

As the New Look was elaborated in theory and practice it became a package of interrelated concepts, some military, some political. Its point of departure was the need to maintain military forces for the long pull without accepting any particular target date for complete military readiness. It placed emphasis upon the new weapons of mass destruction as the basis for providing the retaliatory striking power needed as a deterrent to any aggression, large or small. It favored a reduction of U.S. forces deployed overseas in order to create a central reserve of strategic reserves on U.S. territory. Army forces would be kept small lest we be tempted to use them to fight another Korea by conventional means. The partisans of the New Look were convinced that the U.S. should never again make that mistake and set about reducing Army forces to make it physically impossible even if our future leaders might be so inclined.

The adoption of the New Look was one of the most significant actions of the new Eisenhower Administration. It established the direction which United States military policy has followed from 1953 to the present day. Its immediate effect was the reduction of personnel strengths for the armed services for the Fiscal Years 1955 and 1956 and a sharp increase of the size and level of modernization of nuclear air forces at the expense of the conventional forces.

A first step in the implementation of the New Look was to change the composition of the Joint Chiefs of Staff. President Eisenhower in his press conference of May 14, 1953, stated that he had decided to make this change as a demonstration of his Administration's new approach and its severance of ties with the past. The new appointments were Admiral Arthur Radford replacing General Omar Bradley as Chairman of the Joint Chiefs of Staff, Admiral Robert Carney for Admiral Fechteler as Chief of Naval Operations,

General Matthew B. Ridgway for General J. Lawton Collins as Chief of Staff of the U.S. Army, and General Nathan F. Twining replacing General Hoyt S. Vandenberg as Chief of Staff of the Air Force.

There were several causes for this simultaneous replacement of the Joint Chiefs of Staff. In the first place, the new Administration looked upon membership on the JCS somewhat differently from the Truman Administration. The new Chiefs were regarded as members of the Administration "team," working for the objectives of that team under the guidance of their civilian superiors. In formulating their military advice, it was hoped that they would take into account the views and feelings of these superiors and avoid submitting contentious or embarrassing recommendations. They were expected to accept public responsibility for the actions of the Administration in the field of military policy, regardless of their own views and recommendations. They were to avoid any impression of disunity in public or before the Congress. That dissent might invoke sanctions was clearly implied by appointing the new Joint Chiefs of Staff for no specified term, with the stated intention to review all appointments after two years. General Ridgway subsequently charged that when he dissented he was subjected to frequent pressure to conform to a preconceived politico-military party line and it was made clear to him that he was not to allow his nonconcurrence to be known to the public.*

There were domestic political reasons for moving out the

* General M. B. Ridgway, "My Battles in War and Peace," *Saturday Evening Post*, January 21, 1956.

old JCS. It seemed illogical to many Republicans to continue to rely upon the military advice of men identified with the military programs which the New Look intended to curtail or abolish. There was also a lurking suspicion that the incumbents in the JCS had not been the neutral military experts that they were expected to be. General Bradley, in particular, was considered suspect. Senator Taft felt that General Bradley had intervened politically in support of the Truman Administration in the matter of sending troops to Europe in 1950-51. In April, 1953, Senator Taft advocated the formation of a stand-by set of Joint Chiefs of Staff who would undertake, even before their formal appointment, a review of military policy. Senator Taft argued that General Bradley and his associates were clearly committed to, and had an intellectual vested interest in, the Truman policies. The Senator had long been opposed to the preferential treatment given the military needs of Europe and, in consequence, was happy to see Bradley replaced by Admiral Radford, who was oriented by experience toward the Pacific and Asia.

Whatever the justification for the mass exodus of the Joint Chiefs of Staff, this event was profoundly disturbing to most professional military men. It suggested that the Joint Chiefs belonged to the Administration in power and were expected to be the spokesmen for its military policy. This concept of role was quite different from that previously accepted. Heretofore the Joint Chiefs had been regarded as a nonpolitical body charged with giving professional advice to the Secretary of Defense, to the National Security Council, and to the President. It had been thought that they should give their advice with limited, if any, attention to political or economic factors, since these components of the national strategy had qualified spokesmen elsewhere in the governmental structure. A new ambiguity was given to the position of the Joint Chiefs of Staff, which has existed to the present time and continues to plague the formulation of our military strategy.

When the new Joint Chiefs of Staff came into office, their first task was to determine the requirements for the implementation of the New Look. In December, 1953, they submitted their estimates in terms of budget and manpower for a stabilized military establishment up to 1957. The military manpower requirements were estimated to be about 2,800,000 men, of which a million men would be in the Army. It was felt that these forces could be supported by an annual defense budget in the neighborhood of $34 billion. These forces and budgets would be adequate only if certain assumptions proved valid, the most important of which was that the requirement for significant U.S. forces in Korea would shortly cease.

The subsequent evolution of our military establishment from 1953 to 1959 is the history of the implementation of the New Look based upon these initial estimates of the Joint Chiefs of Staff in 1953. Its development may be followed in three general areas. The first of these is found in the formulation of basic security policy in the National

Security Council, as expressed in the annual paper of that body entitled "Basic National Security Policy," which provides broad guidance for all the departments of the government contributing to national defense. A second area is the actions of the Joint Chiefs of Staff translating the broad guidance of the National Security Council into specific plans and programs to produce the military forces necessary to support the approved national policy. The basic JCS document for this purpose is called the "Joint Strategic Objectives Plan" (JSOP). The final area is in the activities related to the formulation of the annual defense budget, where the allocations of financial resources are made to support the plans and programs of the JCS and the military services. In all three areas the New Look was to encounter difficulties which will be the subject of the next two chapters.

CHAPTER III

THE NEW LOOK IN ACTION, 1953-1956

FROM ITS inception, the Army had never been happy with the New Look, which its representatives accepted initially with many misgivings and reservations and eventually rejected. Shortly after assuming office in 1953, General Ridgway, the Army Chief of Staff, found himself frequently in a minority of one against the other Chiefs in matters relating to the implementation of the New Look program. His courageous opposition, which he felt obliged to maintain against the majority view, eventually brought him into official disfavor and led to his retirement two years later in 1955.

It was not the emphasis and favor bestowed upon air power which aroused Army misgivings with regard to the New Look. The experience of the events in Korea was far too clear in the minds of the leaders of the service which had paid the preponderant price in lives and resources in the frustrating operations of that war. They perceived in the restrictions placed upon our armed forces in Korea a sharp reminder of the importance of political factors as determinants of the decisions of civilian leadership in time of crisis. Was it realistic to assume the unrestricted use of atomic weapons in future military operations, as predicted in the New Look? The Korean experience suggested "no," and subsequent events were shortly to justify concern over placing too great reliance on weapons of great destruction as the principal response of our armed forces. Indeed, the ink was hardly dry on the New Look before the episode of the fall of Dien Bien Phu provided a practical test of the efficacy of the New Look strategy and exposed its weakness. The deteriorating situation of the French defense there in early 1954 led to discussions in the Pentagon and White House in April and May of the nature and degree of possible United States intervention. Although some exponents of air power urged intervention by aerial bombing, largely through General Ridgway's efforts the fact was eventually accepted that any intervention by that time would be either too late, too little, or of the wrong kind. In particular, it was doubted that any air attack could be mounted on a sufficient scale to offer hope of success without, at the same time, endangering the French defenders. During these deliberations and hesitations, the need was apparent for ready military forces with conventional weapons to cope with this kind of limited-war situation. Unfortunately, such forces did not then exist in sufficient strength or in proper position to offer any hope of success. In May, Dien Bien Phu fell and in the following July in Geneva, Indochina was partitioned between Communism and Freedom at the 17th Parallel. This event was the first, but not the last, failure of the New Look to keep the peace on our terms.

In spite of the lesson of Dien Bien Phu added to that of Korea, in 1953 and throughout 1954 the U.S. military forces were progressively adjusted to the New Look pattern through the working of the successive defense budgets. In the meantime, at home and in the USSR, important progress was being recorded in the development of atomic weapons. The United States revealed the development of a megaton weapon in the 1952 Eniwetok test. The release of this information was followed in August, 1953, by news of a Soviet hydrogen explosion. Although the Soviets were known to have exploded an atomic device in 1949, up to this time we had belittled the achievement on the ground that it was a mere explosion, not an operational weapon. Now it was clear that the Soviets were well along in nuclear progress and for the first time there was discussion of the effect of the eventual loss of the U.S. atomic monopoly and of the possibility of an era of mutual deterrence. By this was meant a stalemate in atomic destructive power in the East and the West which would deter both sides from deliberately choosing general atomic war in any conflict of interests.

It is curious that the possibility and implications of mutual deterrence had not affected defense thinking sooner, since the first Soviet nuclear explosion preceded the Korean War by nearly a year. But in dedication to the appeal of the "absolute weapon," our leaders had ignored, or affected to ignore, the political disadvantages of large-yield nuclear weapons and the obvious fact that they are inapplicable to lesser conflicts. It was from unofficial critics of national defense that the public was first to receive intimations of the limitations of dependence on a nuclear strategy. Among the writings on the subject was George F. Kennan's 1954 book, *The Realities of American Foreign Policy*, in which he stated that "the day of total war has passed. . . . from now on limited military operations are the only ones which could conceivably serve any coherent purpose." Articles in a similar vein appeared over the signatures of B. H. Liddell Hart, W. W. Coffman, Vannevar Bush, and Bernard Brodie. Such articles from unofficial sources represented the first public questioning of the validity of the New Look policy of Massive Retaliation and I welcomed them warmly. Their acuity was all the more remarkable from the fact that the authors did not have access to complete information with regard to atomic weapons effects.

Behind the closed doors of the Executive Department of the government, a school of doubt was beginning to challenge the New Look strategy. The evidence of the Soviet progress in the nuclear field made it impossible to ignore the fact that the world power situation was undergoing an important change. In January, 1955, the National Security Council made its first comprehensive review of the 1953 statement of the New Look. In the course of this review, recognition was given for the first time to the possibility of a condition of mutual deterrence and the importance in such a period for the United States to have versatile, ready forces to cope with limited aggression. Otherwise the country might sometime have to choose between yielding to local aggression or applying the undiscriminating power of nuclear destruction. In retrospect, the conclusions of this 1955 review represented a most encouraging trend away from reliance on Massive Retaliation and provided what appeared to be authoritative guidance in support of a more flexible strategy.

Army leaders found great hope in this new 1955 guidance. I received a copy of it in my headquarters in Tokyo shortly before my return to the United States to succeed General Ridgway as Chief of Staff. In February, 1955, in the course of the discharge of my duties in Korea and Japan as Commander of Army Forces in the Far East, this new assignment had caught me by surprise. I was inspecting an element of the 1st Cavalry Division in Japan on February 18 when a messenger from my headquarters in Zama handed me a cable from Army Secretary Robert Stevens asking me to return at once to Washington for consultation. As General John E. Hull was about to retire from his post as Commander in Chief, Far East, I suspected that the recall related to my taking over that assignment. At the same time, I was aware that the difficulties General Ridgway was having as Chief of Staff were creating rumors that he might retire. These circumstances caused many speculations in the Taylor household on the eve of my departure. Like any

Army wife faced with the possibility of a move, Mrs. Taylor demanded that she receive immediate word of any such development in Washington. So like conspirators, we worked out a domestic code for clandestine communication. If I were to take over General Hull's post I would cable, "Lucille [Mrs. Hull] sends regards." If it were the Chief of Staff assignment, the message would be "Penny [Mrs. Ridgway] sends regards."

Arriving in Washington, I was met by the Deputy Chief of Staff, Lieutenant General Walter Weible, who assured me that neither he nor General Ridgway knew the purpose of my return, that only Secretary Stevens could inform me. The next day I saw the Secretary for the first time but did not get a complete answer to my question. He indicated that I had been called back primarily to discuss succeeding General Hull but that something else might be in the background. Although a bit mystified, I wired Mrs. Taylor, "Lucille sends regards."

On the following day Mr. Stevens took me to see Secretary of Defense Wilson. As was his custom, Mr. Wilson did not get down to brass tacks at once but approached the real issue by way of a long, rambling discussion of conditions in the Orient. He then began to cross-examine me on my readiness to carry out civilian orders even when contrary to my own views. After thirty-seven years of service without evidence of insubordination, I had no difficulty of conscience in reassuring him, but I must say that I was surprised to be put through such a loyalty test. After these preliminaries, he then opened up and revealed that I was being considered by the President as a successor to General Ridgway and that he, Mr. Wilson, was looking me over to see if I would do.

Apparently, I passed this test because later he told me to call on the President at 2:30 P.M., February 24. This I did. It was my first meeting with my old wartime commander since he had become President. He greeted me with his customary warmth but there were serious matters on his mind. He wished to be sure of the attitude of the prospective Chief of Staff. He went over essentially the same ground as Mr. Wilson with regard to loyalty to civilian leadership. His manner of expression was different but the purport was the same. Again I had no trouble in responding without reservations. Again I apparently passed the test— still hardly knowing why it had been given. As I left, the President indicated his intention to nominate me to succeed General Ridgway after a short tour of duty in General Hull's post of Commander in Chief, Far East.

Returning to the Pentagon, I wired, "Penny also sends regards," thereby creating utter confusion in my home at Zama.

It was following my return to Japan that I first saw the 1955 text of the "Basic National Security Policy." Struck by the breadth of its language and the degree of departure from the dogma of Massive Retaliation, I developed prior to my return to Washington the first draft of a paper entitled "A National Military Program," which provided the outline for a military program for carrying out the National Security Council guidance as I understood it. After becoming Chief of Staff, I gave the original paper to the Army Staff for criticism and refinement. The resulting changes were minor and the document was approved by Army Secretary Wilber M. Brucker (who had succeeded Secretary Stevens on July 21, 1955) as a statement of the kind of military program we felt the country required during the coming years. As such it was the first coherent statement of the new strategy of Flexible Response which was taking form to oppose the orthodox strategy of Massive Retaliation. As it is basic to the argument of the book, the entire document is reproduced below.

1 October 1956

A National Military Program

1. *Objectives of a National Security Program.*

The basic objective of the U.S. national security policy is to preserve the security of the U.S. and its fundamental values and institutions. In furtherance of the basic objective, the U.S. seeks, by any and all means acceptable to the American people, to alter the international Communist movement to the end that it will no longer constitute a threat to the national security of the U.S. The National Security Program must include national programs in political, diplomatic, military, economic, psychological, and cultural fields which contribute to the stature and prestige of the U.S. and to the attainment of its national objectives. Its central aim is the deterrence of Communist expansion in whatever form it may take. The U.S. must have the political, military, economic, and moral strength sufficient to induce the Communist Bloc to renounce or refrain from all forms of aggression. The evidence of this strength must be so clear as to create in the mind of the enemy the conviction that aggression will not pay.

2. *Objectives of the National Military Program.*

The National Military Program must be integrated with all the other national programs and have as its basic objective the maintenance of military strength which is capable of dealing with both general war and aggression under conditions short of general war. The military strength of the U.S. and her allies must be so constituted as to prevent war if possible, limit war if it occurs, and successfully defeat any aggression that may threaten the national interest.

3. *Elements of the National Military Program.*

a. The elements of a sound National Military Program must include adequate provision for: deterrence of general war, deterrence of local aggression, defeat of local aggression, and victory in general war conducive to a viable peace.

b. The Soviets have the capability of initiating a general war with an atomic onslaught, possibly with little or no warning, against the U.S. Such an onslaught would be accompanied by other coordinated action to gain Soviet objectives on the Eurasian land mass. It is fundamental, therefore, that the United States Military Program make provisions for the deterrence of this type of war.

c. While this all-out atomic war initiated by the Soviets

presents a very grave threat, aggression short of general war appears more likely to occur than deliberately initiated general war. In the approaching era of atomic plenty, with resulting mutual deterrence, the Communists will probably be inclined to expand their tactics of subversion and limited aggression. The National Military Program, therefore, must provide for the deterrence of limited aggression, and for the defeat of such aggression if deterrence measures fail. Otherwise, any of the following may result:

(1) Conflict short of general war may expand into general war.

(2) Continued gains by the Communist Bloc may erode the moral and material strength of the Free World with consequent loss of the capability to deter local and general war.

(3) A large part of the Free World may either fall to local aggression or so incline to neutralism as to leave the United States in a virtual state of isolation.

(4) Repeated success in creeping aggression may encourage a Communist miscalculation that could lead to general war.

d. The possibility must always be recognized that in spite of all our efforts at deterrence, general war, in which atomic weapons will be used from the outset, may occur and last for an indeterminate period. The U.S., therefore, must be prepared for such an eventuality and the National Military Program must provide for the rapid expansion essential to the successful conduct of general war.

4. *Military Requirements of the National Military Program.*

The requirements of a military program developed in consonance with paragraph 3, above, are:

a. The maintenance of military technological superiority over the Communist Bloc.

b. A deterrent, atomic delivery system capable of effective retaliation against an enemy.

c. A continental defense system, including both active and passive measures, strong enough to prevent an enemy from delivering a crippling blow to the Continental United States.

d. Adequate Army, Navy, and Air Force forces deployed abroad to meet our international obligations, and backed by logistic support adequate for sustained combat.

e. Ready forces of the Army, Navy, and Air Force capable of intervening rapidly in areas where local aggression may occur. These ready forces should have the capability of employing atomic weapons when and to the extent authorized by proper authority. The logistical back-up adequate to support these forces in combat should be immediately available.

f. Other ready forces of the Army, Navy, and Air Force, in being, capable of rapidly reinforcing the forces in "e," above, under conditions short of general war and the forces in "d," above, in the event of general war. These other ready forces should have the capability of employing atomic weapons when and to the extent authorized by proper authority. The logistic arrangements should be capable of supporting these forces in either an atomic or nonatomic local war and in an atomic general war.

g. Military and economic aid programs capable of developing indigenous strength and confidence among our allies and of assisting in the deterrence and defeat of Communist aggression.

33

h. Reserve forces in the United States capable of rapid mobilization to:

(1) Replace ready forces in "f," above, committed against local aggression.

(2) Meet the needs of an atomic general war.

i. Stockpiles of equipment for the United States and selected allies necessary to meet the requirements of war until wartime production becomes adequate.

j. A war-production, mobilization and training base to support an atomic general war.

5. *Summary*.

a. Fulfillment of foregoing military requirements constitutes a sound National Military Program. It must, as a minimum, be capable of deterring war, both general and local, and winning local war quickly. In relying on deterrence we must bear in mind that Communist advances in technology and preparedness may render today's deterrents inadequate to restrain the Soviet Bloc tomorrow.

b. The National Military Program must be suitable for flexible application to unforeseen situations. It cannot be geared to any single weapons system, strategic concept, or combination of allies. It must be capable of supporting our national policy in all situations. It should attract essential allies and not repel other allies. In short, the military program of the United States should include all reasonable measures to prevent general and local war and at the same time contain the potentiality of waging any war, large or small, in such a manner as to achieve our national objectives and to bring about a better world upon the successful conclusion of hostilities.

This document is noteworthy for its unqualified assertion that the deterrence of war is the primary objective of the armed forces. It recognizes deliberate general war as a grave threat but, in view of the implications of a situation of mutual deterrence, it rates deliberate general war as less likely than lesser forms of aggression. Under such conditions it is extremely important to be able to cope quickly with limited aggressions since, if unopposed, they will lead to the attrition of our world position or, if resisted with inadequate means, they may expand into that general war which we are most anxious to avoid. If we act in consistence with the principle of deterrence, we should make ample provisions for those forces contributing to the deterrence of general war, the deterrence of local aggression, and the defeat of local aggression before seeking to satisfy the full requirement for survival or victory in general war. Personally, I doubt that this latter requirement can ever be determined, much less satisfied.

The acceptance of such priorities of effort would have resulted in added attention to so-called limited-war forces and would have placed them in virtually equal priority with the atomic deterrent forces. It would have given added emphasis to conventional armaments and to the needs for war reserves and a mobilization capability. It would have been a denial of the validity of the short-war concept of the New Look. The stress on flexibility in the organization of our forces to meet the full spectrum of possible military challenges eventually gained for the doctrine contained in the National Military Program the title of a Strategy of Flexible Response.

Army leaders since 1955 have felt that the approval of some such program as the above would be a major step toward meeting the changing requirements of our national defense. It would provide at a minimum the forces to deter war, both general and local, and to win local war quickly. These forces would be of all services—the Army, Navy, Marines, and Air Force would all have an honorable role to play. It would be flexible enough for ready adaptation to presently unforeseen and unforeseeable situations. It would avoid dependence upon a single weapons system and upon a single strategic concept—the capital fault of the strategy of Massive Retaliation. By the ability of our forces to apply graduated force, the program would appeal to our allies, who had little to hope for in Massive Retaliation. All of these factors would provide important advantages to our political leaders in the conduct of our diplomacy at the international council table. Finally, in the unhappy event of war, this flexible strategy would provide military forces capable of achieving military ends without losing sight of the ultimate objective of rational force—the creation of a better world at war's end. Massive Retaliation offers only unlimited destruction with nothing beyond.

This Army paper was first introduced for consideration by the other services at the meeting of the Joint Chiefs of Staff at the Ramey Air Force Base, Puerto Rico, March 3 to 9, 1956. This meeting took place at the direction of

Secretary Wilson to give the Joint Chiefs the opportunity to re-examine in seclusion their 1953 estimate of the long-range requirements of the New Look. My colleagues read this Army study politely and then quietly put it to one side. It was too early to obtain a consideration of fundamental changes at a time when the other services were quite content with the *status quo*. But the issue was only postponed, not settled.

The meeting in Puerto Rico produced little that was noteworthy. The fundamental conflicts between the Chiefs were kept pretty much in the background. The review of the situation was very broad in nature and merely concluded that the military programs being implemented seemed about right if prolonged at planned levels for the next few years. This conclusion meant, in effect, that as stated in the 1953 JCS study, the Army strength should remain at about a million men and the over-all military manpower at around 2.8 million. The Chiefs, however, raised the $34-billion financial estimate of requirements made in 1953, foreseeing the need of an annual defense budget of from $38 to $40 billion in the period up to 1960. In addition to this sum, they felt that an annual military aid program of between $4 and $5 billion would be required.

Later events soon showed that the Chiefs had been too conservative in estimating the mounting costs of the military programs. Secretary Wilson, who joined the meeting at Ramey at its conclusion, was nearer the fact when he suggested that their top figure of $40 billion would soon be

37

exceeded. But this was not a pleasant thought to raise at a time when the Administration did not believe that the country would stand a defense budget of more than about a $36-billion level.

The Joint Chiefs were hardly back from Puerto Rico before the mounting costs of the long-range missiles and bomber programs exposed the conservatism of their estimates of future financial requirements. The concern over the snowballing of defense costs led to the next major conflict revolving around the military strategy. This clash occurred in the spring of 1956 in connection with the drafting by the Joint Chiefs of Staff of the "Joint Strategic Objectives Plan" (JSOP 60) for Fiscal Year 1960. This is the midrange planning document which undertakes to estimate force requirements four years in advance. In the short time since the Ramey meeting, Admiral Radford had become convinced that it would be financially impossible to continue the military programs as planned and that the economies should be made at the expense of the conventional (nonatomic) forces. In particular, he was determined to eliminate from military planning any consideration of the possibility of a conventional war with the Soviet Union. The issue took the form of an argument over the definition of general war and the extent to which the armed forces should count on the use of atomic weapons. I proposed language which would recognize the possibility of some limitations on the use of atomic weapons, particularly in the initial stages of a conflict with the USSR, and the consequent need for conventional forces of significant size. Admiral Radford and the other Chiefs opposed this change, which, if accepted, would have justified greater expenditures for non-atomic forces. In the end, my view was overruled and the definition of general war established as a conflict in which the U.S. and USSR would be directly involved and in which atomic weapons would be used at the outset. The same decision authorized the armed forces to count on the use of atomic weapons not only from the outset of general war but also in situations short of general war when required by military considerations. In effect, these actions ruled out consideration of a conventional conflict of any sort with the USSR and weakened the case for conventionally armed forces in limited wars.

With this victory to support his position, Admiral Radford in July, 1956, led a major effort to cut the conventional forces and particularly the Army. He introduced into the JCS the most drastic proposal of the New Look period, which if adopted would have caused a complete revision of our force structure in the next four years. Although it failed of adoption, the Radford proposal is of historic significance as an indication of the extent to which the extreme partisans of Massive Retaliation were prepared to go. It also illustrates the unhappy position of a military service in an isolated, minority position in the Joint Chiefs of Staff.

Under the Radford proposal, beginning in 1957 the Army deployments in Europe and Asia were to be reduced to small atomic task forces. Resistance to hostile ground attack would be left to these token U.S. forces, supplemented by the indigenous forces of our allies. The Army in the United States was also to be greatly reduced and limited primarily to civil defense missions. The business of fighting limited wars would be given to air and naval forces, with the Marines doing the ground fighting.

The proposal was based upon the unqualified acceptance of the short-war theory. The armed services were to limit their logistic and manpower preparations to the requirements of supporting forces-in-being without making provision for forces to be raised during periods of tension or after the outbreak of hostilities. Thus they would be allowed to buy only the equipment necessary to support the military operations of the active forces organized and trained in peacetime.

The Chiefs met in executive session in Admiral Radford's office on July 9, 1956, to consider the proposal. It was clear to me that the acceptance of the Admiral's plan would destroy the world-wide forward strategy which the U.S. had pursued since World War II, undermine our alliances, and eliminate the Army as an effective instrument of land warfare. Hence, I arrived carefully prepared with a written rebuttal drawn up with the help of some of my ablest staff officers. I took the offensive at the start of the session, attacking the unsoundness of the proposal from all points of view—military, political, and fiscal. The argument was summarized in the following terms: "The Chairman's concept represents a program which prepares for one improbable type of war, while leaving the United States weak in its ability to meet the most probable type of threat. It fixes the form of possible military reaction, with a resultant loss of flexibility and adaptability for the political and military policy of the United States. It will frighten and alienate our friends. It will play the Russian game directed at getting our forces out of Europe and of Asia. It substitutes the concept of 'Fortress America' for our former strategy based upon forward deployment of deterrent forces in co-operation with our Allies of the Free World. I repeat the opinion that it represents an unacceptable military program for the United States."

These words were received in strained silence. The other Chiefs gave me no support, the Chairman undertook no defense. The meeting broke up with no final action, but I left feeling sure that the usual four-to-one split was about to be carried to the Secretary of Defense, where my case would be lost.

That might well have resulted but for help from an unexpected quarter. On July 13, 1956, the *New York Times* carried an article by the late Anthony Leviero, its Washington correspondent, with the headline, "Radford Seeking 800,000 Man Cut." The article went on to describe with reasonable accuracy parts of the proposal which had just been considered in closed session by the Joint Chiefs of Staff. It appeared that Leviero had either benefited from a deliberate leak of information or succeeded in putting together bits and pieces of facts gleaned from contacts with individuals who knew something about what was up. In any case, he had done a very shrewd job of guessing the nature of some of the events taking place in the highest military circles.

This so-called Radford leak created a tremendous hullabaloo in the Department of Defense, in Washington generally, and also had its repercussions abroad. An immediate investigation was started to try to determine the source. The investigation brought nothing to light to permit the identification or punishment of offenders, if such there were. Abroad, the leak was most disturbing to some of our allies. Chancellor Adenauer in particular was very much concerned about the reported proposal to reduce Army forces in Europe. He dispatched at once General Adolf Heusinger, Chief of the German Armed Forces, to discuss the matter with key Defense Department officials. In the meetings following his arrival in Washington, General Heusinger made a very eloquent argument for the indispensable nature of a strong ground shield in Europe as a part of the over-all strategic deterrent. Secretary Wilson assured him that no significant reduction in our European deployments was intended, so that he was able to return to Germany with a reassuring report for the Chancellor.

As a result of this publicity, Admiral Radford's proposal was withdrawn from the JCS and all copies of it in written form were recalled to the office of origin. The critical danger to our overseas deployments and limited-war forces was laid for the moment. It was to reappear, however, a year later in slightly attenuated form in the Wilson-Radford program for the military forces in the period 1957 to 1961.

One characteristic of this period was the effort of the Department of Defense and the State Department to keep secret the struggle which was going on within the Joint Chiefs of Staff over Massive Retaliation and related issues. Although the Army paper, the "National Military Program," became an unclassified document, I ran into serious difficulties when I undertook to write an article outlining the thinking contained within it. I had been invited to make this effort by Mr. Hamilton Fish Armstrong, the editor of *Foreign Affairs*, who was aware of the nature of my views from discussions in New York in the Council on Foreign Relations.

In draft form, the proposed article was entitled "Security Through Deterrence" and undertook to outline in a deliberately low key the reasoning behind the Army's views of the National Military Program. Recognizing that the program might be called a strategic catch-all creating impossible dollar requirements, I stressed the need for putting our money on forces contributing to deterrence and then, only after meeting their needs, on forces and programs for use only in case deterrence failed. The concluding paragraphs of this article ran as follows:

Faced with the decisions which would flow from a lack of faith in deterrence and from a fixation on the requirements of survival in general atomic war, our national planners will, it is hoped, choose to support the flexible program of deterrence outlined above. If so, they will insist upon first making adequate provision for those forces which clearly contribute to deterrence, allocating only whatever can be afforded thereafter for hedging against the failure of deterrence. Thus, we will live with some risk, but in a way which seems preferable to a dreary existence in caves and deserts, the prospect offered if we act consistently with the assumption that the only war worth preparing for is surprise, nuclear attack on the United States.

In contrast, the military program of deterrence recommended herein has flexibility to cope with various forms of military action. It is geared to no one weapons system, to no fixed concept of future war. It is not blind to the awful dangers of general atomic war; indeed, it takes as its primary purpose the avoidance of that catastrophe. At the same time, it makes due recognition of the need to cope with situations short of general war. It undertakes to maintain a forward posture designed to keep war as far as possible from our shores. It should reassure rather than repel allies. Most important, it will permit our national leaders a wide range of choice when at some future critical moment of history they must determine the appropriate military reaction required by our national interest.

When this article was presented for clearance it ran into trouble in both Defense and State. In Defense it was referred to Admiral Radford's office, following the practice of the Secretary of Defense to enlist the help of the Chairman to keep the public statements of the Chiefs in line with departmental policy.

The reply which I received was over the signature of the

Assistant Secretary of Defense for Legislative and Public Affairs. It declined clearance on the grounds that my views were in conflict with approved policy, that they should be argued out before the JCS and not in public, and that their expression could seriously jeopardize our international relations.

State was also unhappy, but for different reasons. In stating the case for a probable increase in limited aggressions on the part of the Soviets, I had commented that their rather encouraging past successes in the fields of infiltration, subversion, and local aggression would lead them to continue these tactics. State's censor wrote, in objecting to this comment, "The United States line has been that their [the Soviets] aggressive methods have been at least temporarily abandoned because of their failure."

It mystified me then, as it does now, just what "failure" the State Department had in mind. Was it the bloody stalemate in Korea or the painfully slow reduction of the Communist guerrillas in Malaya? If so, on the other side of the coin, Communism had gained all of China except Formosa and this victory was perhaps the most significant political event since World War II. North Vietnam had been overrun and the safety of the southern part was in continuing danger. Increasingly tough language from the Kremlin was revealing growing Soviet confidence arising from the possession of increasing numbers of atomic weapons. All this in the aggregate did not look like Soviet failure.

In other comments, the critics in State tried to follow the

orthodox line but were trapped in its inconsistencies. We should admit, they felt, to no weaknesses in our reliance on atomic weapons and our faith in their deterrent effect. There should be no doubt as to our determination to use the big atomic weapons in retaliation against all-out aggression, but we would not *initiate* atomic warfare. Left unanswered was what we should do if our opponent also did not initiate atomic warfare but committed his aggression through conventional warfare.

Faced with this opposition to my article and knowing the futility of an appeal to the Secretary of Defense, I dropped the matter. If the reader wishes to see it in its entirety, with the reviewer's comments, it is found in Appendix A. It is of interest now primarily as an indication of the efforts at the time to conceal the existence of the deep schism in the JCS and the growing doubts about Massive Retaliation. Such an attitude might have had some justification if all spokesmen for both sides of the issue had been equally restrained while a serious effort was being made to decide the issue. Unfortunately, no such action was taken to settle the issue of principle, while year after year the effect of the defense budgets was molding our strategy into an unchangable pattern.

Although, bit by bit, evidence of the existence of a serious problem trickled out, it was not until the publication of the testimony of the Joint Chiefs of Staff on the 1960 budget before Congressional committees that the full extent of the basic disagreement became apparent.

CHAPTER IV

THE NEW LOOK AGES, 1956-1959

FROM the summer of 1956 on, the primary concern of the Department of Defense continued to be the mounting costs of the missile and heavy weapons programs. It became clear that these programs, if carried forward as initially planned, would generate costs in subsequent years far beyond the level of feasible budgets. However, the events in Hungary and Suez in late fall made it impossible to think of military force reductions. Hence, in the fall of 1956, the Army, in preparation for the 1958 budget, was allowed to continue to plan on a strength of a million men. Shortly after the turn of the year, however, concern over military events in Europe and the Middle East subsided while budgetary problems continued to mount. In February, 1957, the services were told that they could anticipate a $38-billion defense budget for Fiscal Year 1958, which would require a 10 per cent reduction in military personnel. This meant the Army going from a million men to 900,000.

Meanwhile, in both 1956 and 1957 the National Security Council performed its annual review of the basic military policy. It is difficult to say what effect budgetary concerns

47

had upon these revisions, but it is a fact that they were far more favorable to the strategy of Massive Retaliation than had been the 1955 edition. I felt that they tended to encourage increased dependence upon the use of atomic weapons and watered down the references to forces with flexible and selective capabilities. They gave support to the short-war concept by setting limits to the preparations which the armed services could make to meet the needs of the early months of conflict. Finally, they modified the definition of limited war to introduce the thought that it was a form of military conflict occurring only in less-developed areas of the world, to be coped with by limited United States forces. Such language gave aid and comfort to the partisans of Massive Retaliation, which the latter were prompt to exploit in developing the Fiscal 1959 budget.

The issue came to a head in a dramatic meeting of the National Security Council on July 25, 1957. Although during the spring the Soviets had directed threats and warnings at Norway, Denmark, Greece, and Iceland over the consequences of harboring Western troops and bases, the summer was a comparatively quiet period. Hungary and Suez were in the background of 1956; the shock of Sputnik I was yet to come in October of 1957. This short period of freedom from crisis was deemed opportune to propose a reduction of military forces somewhat along the line of the abortive Radford proposal of the previous summer. Recognizing, no doubt, the impossibility of obtaining the concurrence of all the Joint Chiefs of Staff, Secretary Wilson decided to produce virtually singlehanded a long-range program for presentation to the National Security Council. In preparing this plan, he reportedly depended upon Admiral Radford, Deputy Secretary Quarles, and Brigadier General Carey Randall of the Marines, his personal military assistant. In any case, the Joint Chiefs had no hand in it.

Whatever the precise authorship of the program, it hit the armed services like a bombshell. The Service Secretaries and the Chiefs of Staff learned of its existence only three days before its presentation for approval to the National Security Council. It covered the period 1959 to 1961, and undertook to hold the annual defense budget at approximately $38 billion by reducing military manpower to compensate for the rising cost of military equipment. Specifically, the over-all military manpower was to decrease from 2,500,000 men in 1959 to 2,200,000 men in 1961. The decline in strength was to be particularly sharp in the Army, which would drop from 900,000 to 700,000 men and from 15 to 11 divisions in the three-year period.

Army Secretary Brucker and I first became aware of the existence of this program at the meeting of the Armed Forces Policy Council on July 22. Viewing it as the effort of the Wilson-Radford leadership to set the national strategy even more deeply in the concrete pattern of Massive Retaliation, we prepared to meet the issue head on before the National Security Council. As I saw the world situation, there was no justification whatsoever for any cutback in military manpower—the Soviet threat was on the rise, not on the wane. If the proposed cuts were made, it would be impossible to maintain our overseas deployments and to discharge our commitments to our allies in Europe and the Far East. With these sobering thoughts in mind, I prepared my part of the rebuttal of the Department of Defense program.

The meeting of the Council on July 25 thus became the scene of a major debate before the full membership of the National Security Council under the chairmanship of the President. Brigadier General Randall made the presentation for the Secretary of Defense, using charts and graphs to show the proposed trends of our military forces during the period under consideration. When he finished, the Service Secretaries and the Chiefs of Staff were asked for their views, the Army leading off as the senior service. My statement, which had been co-ordinated with that of Secretary Brucker's, expressed deep concern over the plan to reduce the personnel and combat units of all services, and particularly of the Army. Under the Wilson plan, the budgetary savings resulting from reduced manpower were to be spent for further investments in the heavy, costly equipment of use only in general atomic war. There was to be no significant modernization of those forces necessary not only in general war but in lesser wars where the big weapons could not be used. This increased emphasis on preparation for all-out nuclear war seemed particularly unjustified at a time when it was generally agreed that the order of probability of future military challenge was: first, cold war;

second, military conflict short of general war; finally, general war.

Disregarding this estimate of probability, Secretary Wilson's program concentrated on the requirements of the big atomic war and failed to provide the tools to meet quickly and decisively armed aggression short thereof. These aggressions, if not quickly suppressed, might lead to the devastating nuclear war which it was our main purpose to prevent. It was all too clear, I concluded, that the constant downward trend in ground forces would lead to the eventual abandonment of a forward strategy and to the undermining of our system of collective security. At the same time, we would lose still further the ability to react swiftly and effectively to the most likely form of military challenge—limited war—and run the hazard of permitting the erosion of our cause or of blundering into general war.

After all the services had spoken, Secretary Wilson, obviously chagrined at the evidence of open dissent in his official family, conceded that his program would have an especially adverse impact on the Army, but said it was based upon the approved policy to "maximize air power and minimize the foot soldier." If this were not the military policy of the United States, then he would concede that the program was without foundation.

I waited for someone at the Council table to challenge these words of the Secretary of Defense, but no voice was raised to gainsay their accuracy. There seemed to be tacit agreement that this was a correct if colloquial statement of the military strategy being pursued by the United States. Admiral Radford interjected a remark that the program was merely a logical extension of the New Look—which indeed it was. Then the discussion shifted to whether the country would stand for a $38-billion budget—which some members were inclined to doubt. There was no consideration of the fundamental soundness of the background strategy of the Defense program.

This program in its entirety was never specifically approved or disapproved. Nevertheless, it remained the objective of the Department of Defense and served as the point of departure for the 1959 budget. The Army was told to plan on an end strength of 900,000 men for Fiscal Year 1958, and 850,000 for end Fiscal 1959. *All the services were given money ceilings in terms of expenditures rather than in obligations,* as had been formerly the case. This change required a new system of bookkeeping, for which the services were not prepared. In the following year, this new system came to restrict the services severely in the efficient use of their funds. From the point of view of the Bureau of the Budget, the expenditure ceilings had the advantage of protecting the Treasury from calls upon its cash reserves for which provision had not been made. In spite of these ceilings and restrictive directives, when the Army presented its budgetary requirements to the Secretary of Defense in November, both Secretary of the Army Brucker and I defended the need for a 925,000-man army with fifteen divisions rather than the 850,000, thirteen-division force supportable under the Wilson directive. At the same time, we received an unexpected, though temporary, assist from the Russians.

In the same way as the events in Hungary and Suez in the fall of 1956 had protected the strength of the military services, now in October, 1957, the success of the Soviet satellite, Sputnik, proved a valuable ally in maintaining personnel levels and obtaining additional funds. However, since Sputnik was primarily evidence of Russian progress in heavy missiles, it brought budgetary support mainly to the strategic delivery forces of the Air Force and of the Navy. The Joint Chiefs of Staff were invited on November 11, 1957, to prepare for the Secretary of Defense a list of high-priority items not provided for in the basic 1959 budget for which they recommended additional financial support. On November 17, 1957, they unanimously recommended a list which totaled about $1.5 billion. Most of the items were for the benefit of the long-range missile programs, of the Strategic Air Command and of antisubmarine warfare forces—in short, of general atomic war forces. As an exception, the Joint Chiefs recommended $362 million for the Army, to permit it to retain a strength of 900,000 and to accomplish limited modernization. This was the one and only time that I ever received support from my colleagues to increase the strength of the Army, and I was understandably jubilant. But there is a jingle bearing on Pentagon life which says:

> Nothing is complete,
> Neither victory nor defeat.

Such proved the case with this apparent victory in obtaining additional funds for the Army and for the reinforcement of our limited-war capability. The Department of Defense subsequently cut the $362 million unanimously recommended by the Chiefs to $198 million and the personnel strength to 870,000 men. The Bureau of the Budget reduced the money further to $146 million, the figure eventually accepted by the Congress, of which $88 million was for Army modernization. This gain for modernization proved to be illusory, however, as the Department of Defense then reduced the Army budget by essentially the same amount in another essential account to pay for this item. Thus, the only real gain from the entire transaction was $58 million, of which $30 million was to support a 870,000 man strength and $28 million was for additional research and development. Army modernization requirements were to be "absorbed," in the jargon of the Pentagon bookkeepers, who, in this case, had proved themselves more powerful than the united front of the Joint Chiefs of Staff.

In its final form, the new budget projected forward the old trends of the New Look. The percentages of the budget by service and function remained essentially unchanged. In commenting upon this budget before the National Security Council in November, 1957, I again stressed my concern over the continuing decline in the manpower of the Army and the continuing failure to modernize its equipment. Meanwhile, there were no compensating advantages for our security in the aggregate capability of the other services. The other Chiefs of Staff shared my concern over the reduction in the size of the U.S. military forces and in the rate of modernization in comparison to the two preceding years. They, too, were impressed with the fact that this downward trend in military strength was occurring at a time when the threat to the security of the United States was clearly rising.

During the increasingly heated debates over national security in 1956 and 1957, the attitude of the representatives of the Department of State was one of curious detachment. It was as if they felt that the conflicts in the Pentagon were what the Japanese call "a fire on the other side of the river." However, in the course of the discussions of the 1959 budget, Secretary John Foster Dulles gave for the first time public evidence of loss of confidence in the policy of Massive Retaliation with which his own name had been closely associated. In the October, 1957, issue of *Foreign Affairs* in an article entitled "Challenge and Response in United States Policy," Secretary Dulles made the following significant statement:

During the ensuing years the military strategy of the free world allies has been largely based upon our great capacity to retaliate should the Soviet Union launch a war of aggression. It is widely accepted that this strategy of deterrence has, during this period, contributed decisively to the security of the free world.

However, the United States has not been content to rely upon a peace which could be preserved only by a capacity to destroy vast segments of the human race. Such a concept is acceptable only as a last alternative. In recent years there has been no other. But the resourcefulness of those who serve our nation in the field of science and weapon engineering now shows that it is possible to alter the character of nuclear weapons. It seems now that their use need not involve vast destruction and widespread harm to humanity. Recent tests point to the possibility of possessing nuclear weapons the destructiveness and radiation effects of which can be confined substantially to predetermined targets.

In the future it may thus be feasible to place less reliance upon deterrence of vast retaliatory power. It may be possible to defend countries by nuclear weapons so mobile, or so placed, as to make military invasion with conventional forces a hazardous attempt. For example, terrain is often such that invasion routes can be decisively dominated by nuclear artillery. Thus, in contrast to the 1950 decade, it may be that by the 1960 decade the nations which are around the Sino-Soviet perimeter can possess an effective defense against full-scale conventional attack and thus confront any aggressor with the choice between failing or himself initiating nuclear war against the defending country. Thus the tables may be turned, in the sense that instead of those who are non-aggressive having to rely upon all-out nuclear retaliatory power for their protection, would-be aggressors will be unable to count on a successful conventional aggression, but must themselves weigh the consequences of invoking nuclear war.

These words amounted to the expression of a strong hope that some military solution would eventually be found to permit lessened dependence upon Massive Retaliation. This hope, Mr. Dulles believed, lay in the development of the low-yield atomic weapons of the kind which the Army had been seeking for years. In the spring of 1958, Secretary Dulles pursued this theme in meetings with the Secretary of Defense and the Chiefs of Staff. Most of the Defense officials tried to convince him that our limited-war forces were generally sufficient and our military program needed no drastic revision. Many found the concept of area defense in the NATO territory obnoxious as it contravened the dogma that there can be no limited war in that region. I took advantage of the opportunity of Mr. Dulles's interest to emphasize again the need for expediting the program for small-yield atomic weapons capable of contributing to the area defense which he hoped to realize.

Against the background of these discussions with Mr. Dulles, began the next annual debate over the 1958 version of the "Basic National Security Policy." Coming at a time when the Secretary of State was expressing doubt as to the validity of Massive Retaliation and when rising criticism of this strategy was appearing in editorial and journalistic comments, the debate promised to be particularly important in shaping U.S. strategy. As in former years, the discussion seemed to concern itself largely with words, but the words were extremely important to the makers of military policy.

As the policy review proceeded in the spring of 1958, it was apparent that there would be a major split on the subject within the JCS. The Army, supported this time by the Navy and Marine Corps, held that former statements of basic military policy were inadequate in an era of mutual deterrence and encouraged an undue reliance upon nuclear weapons, particularly upon large-yield weapons, to the impairment of the conventional capabilities of all services. This had been the Army position all along but only of late had it received the support of the Navy and of the Marine Corps. The Navy had been moving toward the Army position for some time, but having a stake in the role of Massive Retaliation, it had been hesitant to support the limited-war philosophy, although inclined to agree in principle. For one thing, the Navy saw the possibilities of the nuclear-powered submarine with under-water-launched missiles and foresaw a new role as a preponderant part of the atomic retaliatory force. But on the other hand, it had a claim on a part of the limited-war mission which it hoped to enlarge. Whatever the reason, by the spring of 1958, the Navy and Marine Corps were ready to join in recommending changes that would take into account the implications of nuclear parity, establish finite limits on the size for atomic retaliatory force, and in general make for a flexible strategy for coping with limited aggression. This new position included recognition of the need to be able to fight limited war with or without the use of nuclear weapons.

The Air Force would have no part of such thinking. It rejected the idea of relative nuclear parity and of mutual deterrence. Some of its spokesmen went so far as to accuse the advocates of the new philosophy of betraying the national interest in conceding the possibility of mutual deterrence. Such talk, they felt, would inspire doubt as to whether the U.S. was prepared to use the weapons in its nuclear arsenal and would prompt misgivings among our allies as to our readiness to support them. For them, the growth of the Soviet nuclear power changed nothing in the situation other than to accentuate the need for more atomic weapons and more delivery vehicles to stay safely ahead of the Russians.

Such was the conflict of views at the outset of the 1958 review of security policy. In the debates bearing on the subject, the Army, Navy, and Marine Corps expounded the point of view, indicated above, that the United States must recognize the implications of mutual deterrence, must be prepared to fight limited war with or without nuclear weapons, and should provide itself with a wide range of nuclear yields. They proposed that common-sense yardsticks should be established to determine the necessary size of the atomic retaliatory forces as well as the forces of continental air defense. They recommended removing from the definition of limited war the inference that such wars would be confined to "less-developed areas" (i.e., outside Europe). Finally, they urged recognition that the United States must be prepared to establish limited objectives to military operations whenever such action serves its interest. Massive Retaliation could not be the answer to everything—perhaps not the answer to anything.

The split in the armed services was carried first to the Secretary of Defense and then to the National Security

Council. Acting as the spokesman for the Army, Navy, and Marine Corps before the Council, I expressed our common feeling of the great importance which we attached to this annual revision of the "Basic National Security Policy." There had been sufficient evidence during the past year of the deterioration of our international power position in relation to that of the Soviet bloc to convince us that a thorough reappraisal of our military strategy was essential.

It seemed hardly necessary to cite in detail the changes in the world situation which imparted urgency to a new statement of national policy. Global events had confirmed the hard facts of the growth of Soviet power, the continued extension of the Communist sphere of influence, and of the impairment of our Western alliances. This trend had been manifested in Communist successes in the Middle East, where they had leapfrogged our mutual security shield of the Baghdad Pact; in Indonesia, where they appeared about to do the same behind the SEATO shield; and in North Africa, where they had a similiar possibility for success around the NATO south flank. These events had been accompanied by our loss of unchallenged superiority in the nuclear field.

I reminded the Council that the Secretary of State had recently indicated his feeling of the inadequacies of continued reliance upon a military policy based largely upon Massive Retaliation. He had suggested the need for a review of our military strategy for the purpose of giving it greater flexibility of application. To permit such a review, the Joint

Chiefs were in need of clear policy guidance to serve as a point of departure. This document under consideration, the "Basic National Security Policy," should provide that guidance. Once it was received, the Joint Chiefs could then appropriately modify the strategic concept upon which we built our military forces.

The over-all problem, as I saw it, was to readjust our strategy to the requirements of living successfully in a period of mutual deterrence. In such a period, it could be assumed that the United States and the USSR would be increasingly restrained from deliberately initiating a general nuclear war except where national survival was directly at stake. In such a situation of nuclear parity, where both sides had the capability of destroying one another, there was no place for a policy of massive nuclear retaliation except as a deterrent to total nuclear war or as a reprisal if one began. This fact had become so apparent that it was doubtful whether either the Soviets or our allies believed that we would use our retaliatory power for anything other than to preserve our own existence.

I urged that we be ever mindful of the attitude of our allies toward Massive Retaliation. Both in NATO and in the smaller nations, there was a growing feeling, I thought, that U.S. military power was becoming increasingly inflexible. By our ever-growing dependence on nuclear weapons and nuclear retaliation as the backbone of our military strength, we appeared to these allies to be reaching the position where we could react to Communist power politics in only two alternative ways—apply all-out nuclear power or back away from the challenge. In the era of mutual deterrence to nuclear war, this inflexible condition of our military strength provided scant support to our political strategy. Our allies doubted, understandably, that we would risk the suicidal possibilities of unrestrained nuclear reaction in order to meet limited military threats.

I reminded the listeners that the foregoing line of reasoning by no means suggested a diminished importance of the maintenance of a powerful atomic retaliatory force. It rather suggested the need for constant modernization and protection of that force as a deterrent shield under which we must always live. However, improved delivery means and higher-yield warheads permitted its reduction in size without reduction in deterrent capability.

As Massive Retaliation ceased to be effective except as a deterrent to general war, there was need for increased emphasis on our military preparations directed at coping with situations short of general war. Under mutual deterrence, limited war itself needed to be redefined as armed conflict in which United States national survival was not directly at stake. This new definition would recognize the possibility of armed conflict in such places as the NATO area, which had been excluded in previous definitions. There was also need for a reappraisal of the requirements of limited war. These requirements were not necessarily for a substantial increase of military forces earmarked for limited wars but rather for the modernization of forces, for the improvement in planning for such situations, for the verification of strategic mobility, and for an over-all concentration of attention on limited war comparable to that which we had bestowed in the past upon general war. It was important, I contended, to present to our allies a picture of instant readiness to respond effectively to challenges short of general war and to eliminate their current impression that we were prepared to respond only with heavy atomic weapons if we responded at all.

In preparing our forces to cope with limited-war situations, I mentioned the great promise of the very low-yield atomic weapons. Until these low-yield weapons should become available in quantity, we would have to depend on the existing tactical atomic weapons, always bearing in mind that in many limited-war situations we would not wish to use atomic weapons at all.

As an outgrowth of a situation of mutual deterrence, it was logical to anticipate an increased level of provocation from the Soviet bloc. We had already seen evidence of increasing aggressiveness since Sputnik and related missile successes. It seemed likely that we would be confronted with increasingly difficult decisions and, hence, it was all the more important that we have available a wide choice of reaction in choosing our future courses of actions.

I closed the presentation stating that the basic issue was the requirement to reorient our military strategy to meet the changed conditions arising from mutual deterrence. In such a situation, our atomic deterrent forces would be the shield under which we must live from day to day with the Soviet threat. This shield would provide us protection, but not a means of maneuver. It was rather to the so-called limited-war forces that we henceforth must look for the active elements of our military strategy. The implication of such a change in strategy was not a vast expansion of forces or an increased expenditure of resources. It was rather a new placing of emphasis, directed at developing a truly balanced system of deterrent forces.

While most of the thoughts contained in this presentation were not new, an exception was the point that limited-war forces had the active role to play in future military operations, the atomic retaliatory forces a passive role. Initially, the concept had been that ground forces in Europe and the Far East were the shield behind which the U.S. could deliver the devastating blows of its atomic sword. Now the role was being reversed. The atomic retaliatory forces had become the shield of protection warding off the threat of hostile atomic attack, while the forces of limited war provided the flexible sword for parry, riposte, and attack. Hence the quality of this sword assumed a new and greater importance.

After I had finished my statement, Generals Twining and White presented the Air Force point of view, which was to retain unchanged the previous year's statement of the "Basic National Security Policy" and hence the *status quo* insofar as our military strategy was concerned. There was animated discussion around the conference table, but to my disappointment Secretary Dulles and his advisers did not provide the strong support for a new strategy which I had hoped. The meeting broke up without a decision being announced but in reality our cause was lost for the time being. Soon after, Secretary McElroy issued a memorandum to the services stating that there had been no changes in the international situation to warrant any significant revision in the text of the "Basic National Security Policy." The eventual decision was to retain the language of the old guidance for the purpose of formulating the 1960 budget, but to keep the controversial parts under continuous review.

The practical effect of this action was to encourage the Department of Defense to design the next budget according to the same methods and procedures as the former ones. It postponed until 1959 the struggle to bring the basic security policy of the government into line with the clearly changed conditions of the international situation. As I write, this task still remains to be done.

Under these discouraging prospects for the proponents of change in national strategy, the formulation of the 1960 budget began in midsummer of 1958 and continued until late fall. The guidelines issued by the Department of Defense were more restrictive upon the services than ever before in the New Look period. In effect, the guidance was directed at maintaining approximately the same over-all dollar ceiling for the defense budget as in 1959 and at retaining the same percentage allocations of resources to individual services. These percentages from Fiscal Year 1955 to Fiscal Year

1959 had been about 46 per cent for the Air Force, about 28 per cent for the Navy and Marine Corps, and some 23 per cent for the Army, with the remainder of the budget going to the Department of Defense itself. In the vital area of funds for the purchase of new equipment, which controls the rate of modernization, the Air Force in this period had consistently received some 60 per cent of the available resources, the Navy and Marine Corps about 30 per cent and the Army about 10 per cent.

To the accompaniment of the Red Chinese guns bombarding the offshore islands in the Taiwan strait, the budget debate carried forward during summer and fall. The renewed evidence of Communist readiness to resort to limited-war measures had no effect on the issue. In the end, the budget went to the National Security Council in December without essential change in the frozen internal pattern of previous years. The only justification for such continued rigidity could have been that world conditions had remained essentially the same since 1954. But had they?

Manpower levels were also maintained as at the end of Fiscal Year 1959. Thus the Army was authorized funds to support an end strength of 870,000, the Navy 630,000, the Marine Corps 175,000, and the Air Force 845,000. In spite of the fact that Congress had put a floor of 700,000 in 1959 under the civilian reserve strength of the Army, the Department of Defense directed the preparation of the budget on the basis of 630,000, a reduction of 10 per cent.

The preparation of the defense budget under these conditions soon ran into serious difficulties. All the services, particularly the Air Force and Navy, had embarked upon long-term, expensive programs for the production of heavy weapons such as the Atlas and Titan intercontinental ballistic missiles, the Thor and Jupiter intermediate-range ballistic missiles, the Polaris submarine-missile system, and the Bomarc surface-to-air missile. The implementation of the early-warning program was creating expenses beyond those anticipated. The Army also had a new program contending for increased funds, the Nike-Zeus antiballistic missile. Thus, to stay within the dollar limits of previous budgets required the elimination or the cutback of many of these expanding programs. In the end it was the IRBM and the Nike-Zeus programs which bore the most significant reductions.

The decision to hold back the Nike-Zeus antiballistic missile program at this time was particularly regrettable. The Army had anticipated the need for such a defensive weapon against missiles shortly after World War II and began serious work on it in 1955. By that time our missile makers had had the experience of developing and producing the Nike-Ajax and the Nike-Hercules antiaircraft missiles and were ready to undertake this new and more difficult task of shooting down the incoming ballistic missile. To them, with their background of experience, the task seemed no more impossible than had appeared the interception of manned bombers in the earlier days of the missile art. They were spurred on by a sense of urgency to provide a defense in time against a new and threatening offensive weapon.

Its need was particularly apparent in view of the U.S. policy not to initiate preventive atomic war, which obliges us to be able to absorb the initial blow from the enemy and still to survive.

At the same time, it was apparent that the USSR was making a major effort in the long-range missile field instead of building a large long-range bomber force as the Air Force had been predicting. There was evidence that this effort was being attended with considerable success, indeed that the USSR was probably doing better in the long-range missile field than the United States. Thus the argument for an expedited antimissile missile program in the United States was difficult to resist and the Army leaders were most earnest in urging such a program.

The Department of Defense and the other services, however, showed little enthusiasm for the Nike-Zeus program. The former foresaw the difficult budgetary problem of providing the funds necessary to expedite production of another expensive weapons system. The other services viewed Nike-Zeus as a rival for defense funds which would be in short supply in 1960 and later. As a result, in the Joint Chiefs of Staff the service representatives, except the Army, recommended the limitation of funds for the Zeus program to the research and development requirements only. My view was that production money should be included in the 1960 budget to permit procurement of long-lead-time items essential for the subsequent program.

A circumstance made it particularly difficult for Secretary McElroy to concur in the recommendation of the majority of the Joint Chiefs of Staff, welcome though it otherwise was. He had previously appointed a scientific committee of members from his own office, headed by Dr. Hector R. Skifter, to make recommendations as to the scope of the 1960 Nike-Zeus program. This committee sided with the view of the Army, recommending $708 million to permit limited production of Zeus equipment. Nonetheless, in the end, the Secretary decided against production money for Zeus in the 1960 budget and limited its progress to continued research and development. This decision imposed a delay of at least one additional year on the operational availability of this unique weapon which is so essential to the deterrence of atomic attack and to national survival if the deterrence fails.

The Joint Chiefs of Staff as a body took no part in the formulation of the 1960 budget—nor had they in previous years. This fact has often surprised the Congress, which always expects the Chiefs of Staff to give them competent advice on the budget. But thus far, the Secretary of Defense has never given the Chiefs as a body a clearly defined role in budget-making. This condition results in part from honest doubt as to the extent to which the Chiefs should be drawn into fiscal matters, in part from a feeling that they would ask for the moon. We had shown the latter tendency no later than June, 1958, when we forwarded to Mr. McElroy an estimate of forces for 1962 bearing a price tag of about $48 billion. This figure was so far removed from fiscal feasibility as viewed by the Secretary that he disregarded the Chiefs' estimate in preparing the budget guidance.

With the Chiefs out of the picture, the budget was put together in the usual way, each service producing its budget in isolation from the others. Although many earnest discussions of uni-service needs took place between the Secretary of Defense, the Department Secretaries, and their Chiefs of Staff, at no time to my knowledge were the three service budgets put side by side and an appraisal made of the fighting capabilities of the aggregate military forces supported by the budget. This so-called "vertical" (rather than "horizontal") approach to building the budget has many defects and accounts in a large measure for the inability thus far to develop a budget which keeps fiscal emphasis in phase with military priorities. It is not an exaggeration to say that nobody knows what we are actually buying with any specific budget. This problem of the budget will be the subject of considerable discussion later.

As the budget neared its conclusion, Secretary McElroy apparently felt the need for some endorsement by the Joint Chiefs of Staff before sending it to Congress. On December 3, 1958, the Joint Chiefs and the Service Secretaries were invited to a stag dinner at the White House. The guests of the President included Vice President Nixon, Treasury Secretary Robert B. Anderson, Budget Director Maurice H. Stans, Mr. Gordon Gray, and Defense Secretary Neil McElroy. We Chiefs had been given to understand that the purpose of the meeting was to allow us to discuss the problems of the new budget with the President. However, it turned out to be quite otherwise.

After an excellent dinner in the main dining room, the President led his guests to the library for talk over coffee. We did not take up budget specifics. Rather, the conversation became a discussion of general economic conditions, the problems facing the Treasury, and the need for greater "team play" on the part of the military Chiefs in connection with the budget. Secretary Anderson made a very able statement concerning the importance of a balanced budget and a stable dollar. Several officials exhorted the Chiefs to give greater weight to economic factors and to assume joint responsibility for the defense budget in the form in which it was about to go to Congress. After receiving something in the nature of a "pep talk," the Chiefs were allowed an opportunity to respond.

When my turn came, I did not argue against the over-all dollar ceiling of the defense budget, but did express my opinion that the planned use of the funds therein would not get the most defense for our money. It was the old case of a fixed percentage division of the funds by service, unchanged from year to year. I repeated again the argument that the rapid technological changes, the new weapons systems, and the changing nature of the Communist threat required a completely new appraisal of our military requirements and the spending for them. No one took an open exception to these views, but subsequent events showed that they had no effect. In the end, the 1960 budget followed the same pattern as the former ones.

Following the meeting at the White House, Secretary McElroy referred the budget for the first time to the Joint Chiefs of Staff with the request for comments, particularly with regard to the feasibility of a further reduction. As the Chiefs could not agree in time upon their reply, the budget was presented to the National Security Council meeting on December 6, with the endorsement only of General Twining, the Chairman of the Joint Chiefs of Staff. He expressed his individual opinion that the budget would provide a sound program for the defense of the nation for the period under consideration.

Immediately thereafter, Mr. McElroy continued to press for the endorsement of the Joint Chiefs of Staff. After much discussion, we finally agreed on the text of the following statement:

MEMORANDUM FOR THE SECRETARY OF DEFENSE

SUBJECT: Joint Chiefs of Staff Position on the Fiscal Year 1960 Budget.

The Joint Chiefs of Staff consider that the FY 1960 proposed expenditure figure of $40,945,000,000 is adequate to provide for the essential programs necessary for the defense of the nation for the period under consideration. They find no serious gaps in the key elements of the budget in its present form, but all have reservations with respect to the funding of some segments of their respective service programs.

72

s/N. F. Twining
—————————————
Chairman, Joint Chiefs of Staff

s/Maxwell D. Taylor   s/Arleigh Burke
————————————————————   ————————————————
Chief of Staff, U.S. Army   Chief of Naval Operations

s/Thomas W. White   s/R. McC. Pate
————————————————————   ——————————————————————
Chief of Staff, U.S. Air Force   Commandant, U.S. Marine Corps

Although this document, in fact, was rather tepid support, the Secretary of Defense elected to declassify it (it had been classified "confidential" by the Chiefs) and to present it to Congress, where it soon became a public document. This action boomeranged, because a close reading of the paper showed that the Chiefs had not supported the specific 1960 budget at all but had stated, in effect, that the over-all expenditure figure would be adequate provided the funds were used pretty much as they individually thought appropriate. Conceding only that nothing of importance had been entirely overlooked in the budget, they indicated reservations about the adequacy of certain programs which, being unspecified in the memorandum, soon became the subject of Congressional query as to their size and nature.

Senator Johnson's Preparedness Subcommittee pounced upon the Chiefs' memorandum and soon called us before the klieg lights of the committee room to express our views of the budget publicly under oath and later to file written statements explaining in detail our reservations. Despite a proper desire to avoid public criticism of our civilian supervisors, our testimony soon showed what we really thought of the budget. Noting the statement that the over-all sum was sufficient but that our individual budgets were far below what was required, one senator dryly remarked that he didn't see how three insufficiencies could add up to a sufficiency. The remark was a good one, but overlooked that fact that there could be excessive expenditures in some areas which, if shifted to remedy insufficiencies elsewhere, might conceivably result in aggregate sufficiency.

The members of the subcommittee knew in advance my convictions on the need for modernizing and otherwise improving limited-war forces and my concern over the continued neglect of the Army. They wasted little time in public questioning but asked me for my views of the budget in writing. As a result, I submitted the following memorandum:

STATEMENT BY THE CHIEF OF STAFF, U.S. ARMY
FOR THE CHAIRMAN, SENATE PREPAREDNESS
INVESTIGATING SUBCOMMITTEE

On 19 January 1959, the Joint Chiefs of Staff submitted a memorandum to the Secretary of Defense, subject: "JCS Position on the FY 1960 Budget." The following statement is to clarify my position, as requested by the Chairman of the Senate Preparedness Investigating Subcommittee, with regard to my reservations with respect to certain Army programs, mentioned in the 19 January memorandum.

The reservations which I had in mind pertain specifically

to four major Army programs. These are: (1) Army modernization, (2) the anti-missile missile (Nike/Zeus) program, (3) the personnel strength of the Active Army and the Reserve Forces, and (4) the Army surface-to-air missile program.

Modernization.

The Army's modernization program is designed to achieve both modernization of the existing inventory and a gradual increase in quantity of inventory to meet the estimated combat and training requirements of the early months of mobilization and of war. The first step each year is to seek funds to replace the average annual inventory loss due to consumption, wearout, and obsolescence. Experience indicates the need to replace annually for these causes about 10% of the current equipment inventory. As the value of the Army inventory is approximately $14 billion, the annual sum required for replacement is about $1.4 billion.

A second requirement is to increase gradually the Army's inventory level from $14 billion to a level of $20 billion, the quantity of equipment which is needed in our supply system to meet the early requirements of mobilization and combat. This level constitutes the Army matériel objective which we wish to attain in a five-year period. Thus, in addition to the $1.4 billion for replacement, the Army seeks another $1.2 billion as an annual increment of a five-year plan to increase the inventory to meet the matériel objective mentioned above, and about $200 million for Industrial Mobilization and Transportation. Therefore, a procurement appropriation of approximately $2.8 billion per year (exclusive of Nike/Zeus) over a five-year period is needed to support this phased program to

75

provide the Army with ample modern equipment. Against this requirement of $2.8 billion, the FY 1960 budget will make available $1.19 billion for procurement and $176 million for Industrial Mobilization and Transportation. The $1.19 billion amount is about $200 million less than the amount required to offset the annual draw-down in inventory due to consumption, wear-out, and obsolescence and makes no provision for building up our present inventory from $14 billion to $20 billion.

My reservation with regard to this program arises from concern over the inability under the FY 1960 budget to make the desired progress in modernizing the present equipment of the Army and in acquiring the necessary additional quantity of matériel.

The Anti-Missile Missile (NIKE/ZEUS).

NIKE/ZEUS is provided sufficient funds in the FY 1960 budget to continue research and development at an optimum rate. It is the only system currently under development which will be capable of defending our retaliatory forces and our vital centers against intercontinental and submarine launched ballistic missiles. No funds are provided to initiate production of tactical equipment and missiles.

My reservation in this area arises from the unopposed ICBM threat and my conviction that the importance of obtaining this unique anti-missile weapon at the earliest possible date outweighs the possible financial risks inherent in initiating selective production now.

Personnel Strength.

During the development of both the FY 1959 and FY 1960 budgets, I recommended that the Active Army be maintained at a strength of 925,000, 15 divisions and the Reserve Components at a paid drill strength of 700,000. The FY 1960 budget will provide an Active Army strength of 870,000, 14 divisions and a paid drill strength of 630,000 for the Reserve Components.

My reservation with regard to the personnel situation in the Active Army is based upon the results of reports and of my personal visits to the principal Army commanders abroad and in the United States, all of whom consider their personnel resources as inadequate to meet in full the requirements of their assigned missions. In order to compensate for the shortage of American personnel, Army commanders in Europe and Korea have been obliged to incorporate large numbers of foreign nationals into combat and support units, thus incurring a heavy dependence upon foreign personnel which might have serious consequences in an emergency.

With regard to the reduction in the paid drill strength of the Reserve Components, my concern is over the adverse effect on the reorganization of the National Guard structure currently under negotiation with State Governors and the adverse impact of the reduction on the readiness of many National Guard and USAR units to meet the desired mobilization time schedule.

Surface-to-Air Missiles.

Army objectives in numbers of surface-to-air missile units for the continental air defense and for air defense in overseas theaters are determined by the Joint Chiefs of Staff after consideration of the recommendations of the Commander in Chief, Continental Air Defense Command, and the commanders of

77

unified commands. The funds for Army surface-to-air missiles in the FY 1960 budget fall substantially short of those needed to reach the goals recommended by the Joint Chiefs of Staff.

My reservation in this field is over the failure to make sufficient provision for these air defense weapons which will be needed for the indefinite future to cope with the high and low altitude threat of the manned bomber and the air-to-surface missile.

This open testimony of the Chiefs of Staff before the Johnson Subcommittee had a country-wide impact. Along with their testimony released from closed hearings before other Congressional committees, it revealed for the first time the extent of the schism within the Joint Chiefs of Staff and the division in their views on Massive Retaliation and related matters of strategy. This revelation profoundly disturbed many members of Congress as well as thoughtful citizens generally. This healthy state of alarm had the benefit of creating a climate favorable to a demand for the re-appraisal of strategic needs which had become so necessary. In the formulation of the 1960 budget, I could see that the Department of Defense intended a similar frozen structure for the Fiscal Year 1961 budget. There was to be no change in the guidance provided by the "Basic National Security Policy." The *status quo* would continue—unless new forces came into play. This changed atmosphere throughout the country promised to make it difficult to stand pat on the strategy and programs of the past. As the strategy of Massive Retaliation came to a dead end in the years 1959 and

1960, we had reached a time for inescapable decisions, the making of which challenged the courage and intelligence of U.S. leadership. To understand the problem of effecting the required strategic reappraisal, it becomes necessary to understand our strategy-making procedure within the government as it exists both in theory and in practice and, in particular, to understand the workings of the Joint Chiefs of Staff.

CHAPTER V

THE MAKING OF OUR MILITARY STRATEGY—THEORY

IN THIS chapter it is not intended to make a detailed study of the organization and functioning of the agencies involved in strategy-making. However, a short digression is necessary if we are to understand the strong and weak points of the present system.

The over-all responsibility for the approval and implementation of our National Security Policy falls to the President. He is assisted by two advisory bodies, the National Security Council and the Joint Chiefs of Staff. The usual members of the National Security Council include the President, Vice President, the Secretaries of State, Defense, and Treasury, the Directors of the Office of Civil and Defense Mobilization and of the Bureau of the Budget. The Chairman of the Joint Chiefs of Staff, who attends as a member of the staff of the Secretary of Defense, is normally the only representative of the armed forces. However, when matters affecting the military services are being considered, it is usual to invite the Service Secretaries and the Chiefs of Staff to the meeting.

The composition of the Council is such that it gathers together the requisite knowledge and experience in the political, economic, psychological, and military fields to permit the broad determination of national objectives and policy. The Council members advise the President as individuals in their own right rather than as representatives of their respective departments or agencies. From their background of experience it is expected that they will seek definitive, statesman-like solutions to the problems of security rather than accept solutions which are merely compromises of departmental points of view.

The Council has two important subsidiary bodies, the Planning Board and the Operations Co-ordinating Board. The Planning Board generally prepares the policy papers which appear on the agenda of the Council. After they are approved by the Council, these papers go to the Operations Co-ordinating Board for co-ordination, implementation, and follow-up on the overseas aspects of the approved policies and programs.

Perhaps the most important action of the National Security Council in the course of the year is the annual review of the "Basic National Security Policy." This is the paper mentioned in previous chapters which undertakes to provide the broad policy guidance for all government agencies involved in national defense. If a reappraisal and reorientation of U.S. military strategy are to be effected, this is the document in which to do it. Despite its portentous character, this document is usually only some twenty-five typewritten pages in length. Its text is often carried forward from year to year with only slight modifications. It contains a broad outline of the aims of U.S. national strategy and a more detailed discussion of the military, political, economic, and domestic elements to support the over-all national strategy. It includes no estimate of the finances necessary to implement the recommended policy and thus has no direct tie-in with the formulation of the federal budget.

The first draft of the annual revision of this document is produced in the Planning Board without direct military participation. However, in the preparation of the paper, drafts are referred to the Department of Defense, the military services, and the Joint Chiefs of Staff. In this way, military views are considered in the preparation of the paper prior to the submission to the National Security Council. The major debates on military strategy reported in preceding chapters have usually occurred at the time of final consideration of this paper by the National Security Council. In its final approved form, the "Basic National Security Policy" should be the blueprint for the security programs of all departments of the government and provide the JCS with a firm point of departure for their strategic planning.

Unfortunately, such is not the case. The end product of the procedures described has thus far been a document so broad in nature and so general in language as to provide limited guidance in practical application. In the course of its development, the sharp issues in national defense which confront our leaders have been blurred in conference and in negotiation. The final text thus permits many different interpretations. The protagonists of Massive Retaliation or of Flexible Response, the partisans of the importance of air power or of limited war, as well as the defenders of other shades of military opinion, are able to find language supporting their divergent points of view. The "Basic National Security Policy" document means all things to all people and settles nothing.

Efficient administration in any field calls for sound advice, clear and timely decisions, and follow-up of the implementation of these decisions. In the NSC, the follow-up is often defective. Although the Operations Co-ordinating Board has limited responsibility for follow-up on overseas operations, it does not follow up on the implementation of the "Basic National Security Policy." While the Department of Defense files periodic progress reports with the NSC, that body never gives a hard look at the actual condition and capability of our military forces at any one time. There is no consideration of the kind and amount of military force we are capable of exerting and its relation to the world-wide obligations which we might have to fulfill. *Nowhere in the machinery of the government is there a procedure for checking military capability against political commitments* or our forces in being against the requirements growing out of the approved "Basic National Security Policy." Similarly there is no procedure to verify that the

83

federal budget is designed to provide the necessary financial support to support the force needed under the "Basic National Security Policy."

Now let us consider the other important agency in strategy-making—the Joint Chiefs of Staff. The latter are a corporate body established by law as the military advisers to the Secretary of Defense, to the National Security Council, and to the President. In practice, the relationship of the JCS to the Secretary of Defense is the controlling one. They approach the President habitually through the Secretary and have no regular contact with the NSC other than through the attendance of the Chairman at Council meetings.

The Joint Chiefs of Staff, as a body, exercise no command but have purely staff and advisory functions. As a staff, they are inserted between the Secretary of Defense and the unified and specified commanders at home and overseas.* They are assisted by a three-star Director and about four hundred other officers drawn from all services, constituting a Joint Staff which operates a military command post on duty around the clock. This is the body which would give military direction to the conduct of war under the authority of the Commander-in-Chief (the President) and the Secretary of Defense. In their staff

---

* Unified Commands: Alaskan Command, Atlantic Command, Caribbean Command, U.S. European Command, Pacific Command, and Continental Air Defense Command.

Specified Commands: U.S. Naval Forces Eastern Atlantic and Mediterranean; and Strategic Air Command.

capacity, the JCS may be described as a committee which performs functions such as are normally assigned to the chief of staff of the commanding general of an operational headquarters. Their effectiveness in such a role has never been tested by the pressures and strains of all-out war but many military men who know the problem are convinced that in such war as the future may hold a committee can never replace a single chief of staff. That is my own opinion.

As an advisory body, the JCS are charged, among other things, with the development of strategic plans and the provision of long-range military guidance for use by the military departments in the preparation of their respective plans. To develop these plans and to provide this direction they need a clear clarion call of guidance from the trumpet of the National Security Council. Otherwise, their own notes will be out of key with the over-all national strategy. Hence, the great importance of the "Basic National Security Policy" paper to the JCS.

The document produced by the JCS which is comparable to the "Basic National Security Policy" in the NSC is called the "Joint Strategic Objectives Plan" (JSOP). Its purpose is to provide planning guidance for the development of the forces needed in the Fiscal Year beginning four years ahead. It estimates the military requirements for cold, limited, or general war, and includes a determination of the military forces together with their dispositions and employment necessary to implement the military strategy derived from the "Basic National Security Policy." It also provides guidance for service mobilization planning and serves as a basis for the annual statement on military requirements to the Secretary of Defense to assist him in developing budgetary guidance for the next Fiscal Year. Thus if the JSOP fulfilled these intended purposes, it would permit timely planning four years into the future and thus would assure that the immediate defense budget contained the funds to initiate the orderly generation of the forces needed. It would trumpet a clear command to the services, which would then know how to play their subordinate parts in contributing to the aggregate of military forces required.

In its usual format, the JSOP contains an intelligence evaluation of the military threat in the period under consideration, a strategic concept for the conduct of cold, limited, and general war, a logistics annex, and a tabulation of forces required to support the strategic concept. It has been the development of the latter, so-called "force tabs" which has generated the greatest divergence of views within the Joint Chiefs of Staff.

Obviously, the JSOP is intended to be a most important document for the orderly development of military programs. Unfortunately, like the "Basic National Security Policy," it has encountered many difficulties in application and has failed to achieve its high purpose. Not one of the three most recent JSOP's has been completed in a form suitable to serve as a true four-year planning document. The primary cause of failure has been the inability of the Chiefs to agree on the best combination of forces supportable by the financial outlays which the Secretary of

Defense has considered feasible for planning. The JSOP was originally conceived as a document which would allow the Chiefs to estimate military requirements without prior consideration of budget ceilings. As a result, JSOP 60 would have required about $48 billion to implement and the later ones $55-$58 billion. Such forecasts were highly unsatisfactory to the Secretary of Defense, who either rejected such estimates or imposed fiscal ceilings to restrain what he considered Blue Sky planning. As a result, the JSOP has become more and more a preview of the next budget squabble and less and less a document for mid-range strategic planning.

Thus, in spite of the seeming logical procedures for developing national strategy in the National Security Council and military strategy in the Joint Chiefs of Staff, the system has failed for several fundamental reasons. The National Security Council has not come to grips with the fundamental defense problems and has failed to produce clear-cut guidance for the armed forces. The Joint Chiefs of Staff have failed to agree on the forces needed to support the agreed strategic concept and hence have not produced the military guidance needed by the military services. The Secretary of Defense has interjected fiscal considerations into midrange strategic planning and has thus deprived it of much of its potential value. But this is only a part of the story. To understand the entire problem it is necessary to look deeply into the Pentagon and see how practice in strategy-making differs from theory. First, let us visit the Joint Chiefs of Staff at work.

CHAPTER VI

THE JOINT CHIEFS OF STAFF
AT WORK

THE Joint Chiefs of Staff meet regularly at ten o'clock on Wednesday and Friday of each week in their suite of offices on the second floor of the Pentagon just inside the River Entrance. Their principal assistants for JCS matters, the so-called Operational Deputies, meet a half-hour in advance of the Chiefs in order to dispose of as many matters of minor importance as possible, then join the Chiefs for the main meeting which follows. These Operational Deputies are generals and admirals of three-star rank who occupy concurrently key positions in the staff of their respective services. In the course of the years they have assumed increasing importance in the JCS system, relieving the Chiefs of many secondary matters and doing the preliminary spadework on major matters prior to consideration by the Chiefs.

The conference room of the Joint Chiefs is about twenty-eight feet long and twenty-four feet wide, with walls painted a particularly disagreeable mustard color, the result of an unhappy choice of paint by the Chiefs on a rainy day in a bad light. The Chiefs seat themselves around a truncated oval table, the Chairman, the Director of the Joint Staff, and the Air Force representatives opposite the Army and the Navy, with the Marine Corps members at one end of the table and two military secretaries charged with keeping the written record of the meeting sitting opposite the Marines. Thus, there are normally twelve individuals at the table, representing the official membership. Outsiders may attend by invitation; indeed, it is quite normal for the Chiefs to call in experts from the Joint Staff or elsewhere to assist in matters within their special competence.

The agenda for a meeting of the Joint Chiefs is usually distributed two days in advance. Agenda items cover a wide range of subjects arising from the broad responsibilities of the Chiefs to the Secretary of Defense and to the unified and specified commands. They include such diverse matters as the long-term plans for the development of the armed services, the personnel and logistic requirements growing out of these plans, the role of new weapons systems and their integration into the armed forces, military aid programs for friendly countries, operational matters affecting the overseas commands, and recommended positions for the Department of Defense on such matters as disarmament, limitation of atomic testing, and similar international questions with which the Department of Defense is concerned.

Each Chief receives a briefing from the members of his

staff on the items of the agenda a few hours before the actual meeting. Called the Indians in contrast to the Chiefs, these service briefers exercise a considerable influence on the ultimate position taken by their superiors. Every Chief has to be alert to the danger of becoming a prisoner of his Indians, who are generally able and enthusiastic young officers trained to defend their views fearlessly before their superiors. I remember a briefing of the Army Chief of Staff several years ago, when the Deputy Chief of Staff, a lieutenant general, was passed a piece of paper during the conference. With a laugh he read it to the group. "If the Chief of Staff tries to change line 2 of page 4, oppose him at all costs. Signed Majors Miller and Mock."

I was an Indian under General Marshall, who taught me the lesson that every Indian regardless of rank was entitled to have his own opinion on any military matter. In the relatively quiet days before Pearl Harbor, as a new major in the office of the Chief of Staff, I took him my first paper for briefing. The world-shaking issue was whether the Alaskan National Guard should have two more companies. I gave General Marshall the staff recommendation and leaned back to receive his decision. "What do you think about it, Taylor?" he asked. I nearly fell off my chair because it never occurred to me that I had a right to an opinion. I never repeated that mistake again. The Indians must have ideas and advance them boldly. But they still should not be allowed to take the Chief captive.

Most of the papers considered by the Chiefs are quickly

disposed of. Others, however, may be carried forward for weeks on the agenda. These are generally the involved papers bearing upon the long-range plans of the services.

The volume of business before the Joint Chiefs is heavy and is becoming heavier. From October 6, 1955, to March 31, 1959, the Joint Chiefs acted upon 2,977 papers. Contrary to the popular impression that disagreement is common in the Joint Chiefs, my record indicates that 2,954 of these papers were unanimously agreed, leaving only 23 in disagreement. The latter, however, represented many of the "blue chip" issues. They included such questions as these:

Should the Army be permitted to have an intermediate-range ballistic missile?

What is the best possible composition of the atomic stockpile in types and yields of weapons?

What authority should be given the Commander-in-Chief of the North American Defense Command?

How should the Pacific Command be organized and staffed?

Should a top priority be given to development of small tactical atomic weapons?

How should the Nike-Hercules and Bomarc surface-to-air missiles be employed?

Is there sufficient troop lift available for limited wars?

Should the "Basic National Security Policy" be modified to place greater emphasis on the possibility of limited war?

Considering the scope of the questions which the Joint

Chiefs do consider, it is interesting to note some of the matters which they might be expected to consider but do not. The first of these is the defense budget, for which they have no agreed responsibility. Although charged with preparing and submitting to the Secretary of Defense statements of military requirements to be used in connection with the preparation of the defense budget, the Chiefs as a corporate body take no part in the budget's actual formulation. However, Secretary McElroy's action in referring the 1960 budget to the Chiefs suggests that the Secretary of Defense has come to feel more and more the need for the endorsement of the Chiefs of his final budget. Since these officers in the past have had insufficient knowledge of the over-all defense budget to warrant an expression of competent opinion, renewed consideration may be expected to giving the Chiefs a more active role in budget-making. Without it, there is no discernible way to align military requirements, the military budget, and the service programs supported by the budget.

Another thing the Chiefs do not do is to make or execute operational war plans. These functions usually belong to an overseas unified or specified commander. Take the case of the landing in Lebanon in July, 1958. The planning and execution of this operation were done by Admiral James Holloway in his capacity as a task force commander reporting to the JCS. The latter approved his plans and saw to it that he had the forces and supplies needed to carry them out. They directed General Lauris Norstad, the Commander-in-Chief, European Command, with headquarters near Paris, to support Admiral Holloway and to provide him with specified forces normally a part of General Norstad's command. They dispatched to him units and supplies from the United States. Then, having verified that Admiral Holloway had a sound plan and the means to execute it, the JCS properly sat back and watched him operate, ready to intervene at any time if he needed help. If war broke out any place overseas today, the role of the JCS would be essentially what it was in Lebanon. However, for a bigger affair, they might have vastly expanded activities at home in initiating mobilization and readying reserve forces to reinforce the overseas commander responsible for the operation.

The Joint Chiefs of Staff organization has the strength and weakness of any committee system. The presence of the active military heads of the services on this committee makes available the broad experience of the responsible military leaders of the nation. Thus, our most important military planning reflects the views of men who know their services, their capabilities and limitations. Their advice to the Secretary of Defense carries the stamp of responsibility and assures the realism of plans made by the men who will be primarily responsible for their execution.

On the other hand, the Joint Chiefs of Staff have all the faults of a committee in settling important controversial matters. They must consider and accommodate many divergent views before action can be taken. In seeking unanimity, they spend much time trying to overcome dissent. For instance, we argued for months before reaching agreement over the allocation by service of the important assignments in the Joint Staff after its reorganization had been authorized by Congress in 1958. When compromise fails, then additional time is required to prepare the contending positions for presentation to the Secretary of Defense. I often felt that we tolerated excessive delay in clearing the day-to-day agenda, probably because a committee rarely has the sense of personal responsibility for the expeditious conduct of business which an individual commander or Chief of Staff feels for the work of his headquarters. Also, since one dissenting Chief can prevent action on an issue for long periods, it is difficult to force consideration of matters unpalatable to one or more of the services. Even when such consideration is directed by the Secretary of Defense, the answer may be "waffled," i.e., made ambiguous or incompletely responsive to the fundamental question.

Unsatisfactory past experience in settling split papers has been an added factor causing delay in coming to grips with important issues. Since their civilian superiors often express acute discontent over receiving split papers which they must then decide, the Chiefs have often been inclined not only to spend excessive time in seeking compromises but even to sweep controversial issues under the rug, where they lie dormant for indefinite periods. A thorny matter, such as the determination of "how much is enough" for the size of the Strategic Air Command and the other atomic deterrent forces, can be and has been sidestepped for years. The proper organization of a military command in the Middle East is another perennial which confronted the JCS when I joined the body and is still unresolved. In partial defense of the Chiefs, the poor record of the decision-making agencies above them has discouraged a forthright effort to set forth the conflicts clearly and to press for their definitive adjudication. In this connection, it should always be borne in mind that the JCS advise; they cannot decide these matters. Decision is the responsibility of civilian leadership.

Since the handling of split views has been a principal obstacle to the effective functioning of the Joint Chiefs of Staff, it is worth while to examine their causes in some detail. It is the common view that divergencies of opinion in the Joint Chiefs of Staff are essentially the result of a narrowly partisan defense of service interests. A close analysis of actual cases will only partially support that opinion. In many cases the divergencies of view spring from far more fundamental and disinterested causes.

A study of cases would reveal that the divergent views of the Joint Chiefs fall generally into three broad categories. First, there are those which are more or less philosophical in nature, arising from the continuing conflict between the strategic concepts of Massive Retaliation and of Flexible Response. These are matters of the kind which should be resolved in the "Basic National Security Policy" document of the National Security Council.

Next, growing out of this background issue are those which relate to the conduct of future war and the ways and means to prepare for it. Within this group are such subjects as the determination of how much is enough for the various kinds of functional forces, the role of new weapons systems in future war, conflicting interpretations of the roles and missions of the individual services, the proper dependence to place upon the use of nuclear weapons, and the optimum composition of the nuclear stockpile.

Below this second level of conflict is a large block of professional and technical disagreements stemming from the broader issues mentioned above. Examples of this third group would include the organization and command of unified and specified commands, specific issues growing out of the twilight zones between the roles and missions of the Army and the Marine Corps, of the Army and the Air Force, and of the Air Force and the Navy. Additionally, there are matters such as the nature and size of Army aviation, the assignment of service responsibilities in continental air defense, command relationships in air-ground operations, and more recently, matters involving operations in space.

From their titles it is apparent that these are not always strictly service issues but often cut across all party lines. Nonetheless, there is an identifiable service position on most important issues which is evident in the discussions and debates in the Joint Chiefs of Staff. At the risk of over-simplification and of incomplete statement, I have drawn up the following tabulation indicating the position of the services as I have understood them on some of the principal issues during the past four years. Their relative length indicates only that I am surer of my ground in writing of the Army than of the other services.

The Army Position

The Army supports the adoption of an over-all strategy of Flexible Response, derived from a complete reappraisal of U.S. strategic requirements in the light of changed world conditions since 1953. As a point of departure for such an appraisal, it urges the establishment by the Joint Chiefs of Staff of agreed standards of sufficiency for strategic retaliatory forces, continental air defense, overseas deployments, limited- and general-war strategic reserves, antisubmarine warfare forces, and similar functional force groupings. Having determined how much is enough, it would then build the defense budget in consistence with the requirements of these functional forces.

The Army regards a certain amount of air defense as an essential part of our atomic deterrent forces. In combination, the atomic delivery capability and continental air defense represent the two components of strategic deterrence, the one offensive and the other defensive, which should be kept in balance to assure the maximum deterrent effect. In view of the growing ballistic missile threat, the emphasis in air defense should shift from a bomber to a

97

missile defense faster than presently planned and the Nike-Zeus antiballistic missile should be made operational as rapidly as possible. Too much money is being spent on the manned interceptor and on the Bomarc missile system. The former is obsolescent; the latter is too late in relation to the waning bomber threat and too doubtful as to technical and fiscal feasibility.

An opponent of the "Fortress America" concept, the Army tends to stress the importance of our overseas deployments and the need for strengthening the ground forces of our principal allies through appropriate military aid programs. It also favors the stockage of forward depots in overseas areas in order to cut down the time of reaction in responding to military situations at a distance from our present deployments in Europe and the Far East.

In developing the need for a strategy of Flexible Response, the Army has become the principal spokesman for increasing the United States capability in limited war. It opposes any thought that the Navy and Marines are capable of taking over this mission which, insofar as it is a form of sustained ground combat, is viewed as a specific Army mission. At the same time, the limited-war mission is not regarded as an Army monopoly, but as one to which all services can and should make a material contribution. For improved joint planning and joint training in limited war, it has favored a single responsible headquarters, possibly by a unified command in the U.S., organized to discharge joint responsibilities in assuring the readiness of limited-war forces.

Concern over the ability to move forces promptly to meet limited aggressions abroad accounts for the intense advocacy by the Army of adequate strategic air and sea lift. Since the JCS have never agreed as to the quantity of strategic lift which is necessary to meet limited-war requirements, the Army urges the establishment of a measure of sufficiency based upon map studies of possible limited-war situations. Also, it favors the predesignation of certain air transport units for planning the movement of spearhead-Army forces, believing that such predesignation would improve joint planning without immobilizing any of the predesignated aircraft. At the same time, there is a need for the modernization of both strategic air and sea lift through a progressive replacement of the obsolescent types of airplanes and ships now in the inventory.

With regard to the forces of the other services, the Army considers that the Air Force is depending too much and too long on manned aircraft, both bombers and interceptors. In view of the tremendous growth in the destructive power of megaton hydrogen weapons, we have today an excessive number of delivery vehicles in the combination of aircraft and missiles now in the strategic deterrent forces. However, this force needs to be modernized through a more rapid replacement of bombers by missiles and its protection improved as necessary through air defense, early warning, and related measures. The thought is that a modernized, well-protected, balanced retaliatory force, while relatively small, would be greatly more effective than the present conglomeration of Air Force, Navy, and allied aircraft, aircraft carriers, and heterogeneous missiles.

With regard to the Navy, the Army accepts the apparent advantages of the Polaris submarine-missile combination but is skeptical as to its time of availability. It views the Navy carrier program as unjustifiably large, while favoring primary attention to the antisubmarine warfare program.

As for the Marines, the Army acknowledges their potential contribution to limited-war situations occurring on or near the coast but resists vigorously any suggestion that the Marines should become a second Army and take over any part of the Army's role of prompt and sustained ground combat.

Finally, it opposes the short-war concept (i.e., that the next war will be over in a matter of hours or days) which is a part of the doctrine of Massive Retaliation and rejects the implications of such a concept upon mobilization readiness. In view of the unpredictable duration of future conflicts, failure to make provision for postmobilization requirements is like the act of a prize fighter who, faced with a fight to the finish, trains for only the first round.

The Navy-Marine Corps Position

The Navy-Marine Corps representatives in the JCS have rather belatedly joined with the Army in supporting the concept of Flexible Response against the advocates of

Massive Retaliation. However, they have shown little enthusiasm for the budgeting by operational functions rather than by service, maintaining that naval forces cannot be broken down into functional categories. They point out that a ship may concurrently contribute to strategic bombing, antisubmarine warfare, and air defense. They are inclined to agree, however, that the present strategic retaliatory forces are probably excessive to their task and should be modernized and reduced in size.

In such a reorganization, the Navy believes that its Polaris submarine missile, with its mobility and concealment, should take over a major part of the offensive strategic retaliatory mission. It would oppose violently any amalgamation of Polaris forces with the Strategic Air Command. Continental air defense receives little support from the Navy. It attempts to restrain large expenditures for this mission, and hence takes a negative attitude toward the Nike-Zeus antimissile missile program.

The Navy, like the Army, opposes the concept of "Fortress America." Although recognizing the need to cope quickly with limited war, the Navy resists planning for any limited-war situation large enough to justify substantial Army forces. Every effort is made to depict the Navy-Marine Corps combination as the answer to the limited-war problem. Consequently, the Navy shows no interest in the strategic air and sea lift requirements of the Army.

The Navy fights hard for the preservation of its present large carrier force, attempting to justify the numbers by the requirements of both general and limited war. While the other services would like to see the Navy concentrate its attention more upon antisubmarine warfare, the Navy prefers to advance along three parallel lines, seeking to expand its role in strategic bombardment and limited ground warfare while retaining its responsibility for antisubmarine warfare.

The Navy agrees with the Army that the short-war concept is dangerous and that reasonable provisions must be made for post-M-Day mobilization.

In general, the Navy-Marine Corps are satisfied with the *status quo* and opposed to any significant changes in the present roles and missions of the services.

The Air Force Position

The Air Force is the service committed to the strategic concept of Massive Retaliation, which it regards as the only valid military strategy upon which to rest our national security. The Air Force spokesmen generally argue as follows:

Massive Retaliation takes "realistic" account of the fact that we can never match Communist manpower on the ground while exploiting our superiority in the air. It is the only effective strategy attainable within our financial means. It forces the USSR to recognize that general war —that is, one in which the U.S. and USSR are direct participants—will be so destructive to them as to represent a totally unacceptable risk. This fear of general war on the part of the Soviets, the airmen believe, will protect the United States not only from general war but from limited war as well, since the Soviets will also fear that any limited war may grow into the general war which would be fatal to them.

Consequently, in the Air Force view, no special preparation is necessary to meet the so-called limited-war threat since it is taken into account by our general war preparations. Indeed, any special preparations might be positively disadvantageous by casting doubt on our determination in a crisis to use our retaliatory power and hence might diminish our deterrent effectiveness. Such doubt would tend to encourage our potential enemies and discourage our allies. We must resist any action which might undermine the credibility of Massive Retaliation.

The Air Force sees our principal danger in the growing strategic air and missile forces of the Soviet Union. To meet this danger, the United States must always keep well ahead of the Soviets in strategic strike capability. To do so we need more and more strategic missiles and bombers, retaining plenty of the latter until the missiles are thoroughly proved. While we would like to assure our strategic strike forces in the U.S. from enemy surprise attack, in strategic air warfare a strong offense is the best defense. Hence the continued growth of the Strategic Air Command (SAC) should take priority over continental air defense, particularly the so-called point defense which the Army provides. Likewise, we should not be misled into large expenditures for antimissile missile defenses, such as the Nike-Zeus system, which are of doubtful feasibility and very expensive. While research and development of an antimissile missile may be justified, we should delay production until a system is proved to work.

The Air Force position on specific issues grows out of the foregoing dialectic. If the argumentation is sound, it follows that budget emphasis should be placed upon general-war forces, specifically upon the Strategic Air Command. Overseas deployments should be reduced to trip-wire forces, and strategic mobile reserves at home limited to relatively small forces. If these are appropriately small, there will be no need to increase the strategic air or sea lift to provide for their movement. Since one needs only to prepare for general war and since general war will be of limited duration, there is no justification for large mobilization stocks in the United States. The mobilization base of all forces should be reduced and the money saved should be placed upon forces in being—preferably air forces.

With the diminution in importance of manned aircraft, the Air Force recognizes a serious problem in maintaining its favored budget position among the armed services. To shore up its position, it is conducting an offensive campaign to take over the Army's mission in continental air defense and a defensive campaign to resist the invasion by the Navy's Polaris of its strategic bombing mission. For reasons not understood, the Air Force representatives have thus far resisted arguments to give mobility to their intercontinental and intermediate-range ballistic missiles. In so doing, they have conceded an important point to the mobile Polaris missile. A belated switch in position may be anticipated.

The foregoing are believed to be reasonably accurate statements of service positions as revealed in the debates of the Joint Chiefs of Staff. The divergencies in these positions suggest the scope and nature of the problems awaiting decision by civilian authority. They also suggest the influence of the budget upon service differences.

The truth is that many service conflicts could be adjusted through compromise but for the knowledge of the fixed size of the defense budget. The fact that there is a ceiling of around $40 billion on the defense budget is a reminder to each Chief that all military programs, however disparate in character, are in fact competitors for a fixed number of dollars. This consideration tends to color the attitude of the individual Chiefs toward the programs of sister services. It tends to make disinterested judgments more difficult than would be the case if it were possible to form judgments without such regard for fiscal consequences. The fixed defense budget, by accentuating the interservice struggle for funds, has become the prime cause of the service rivalry which is undermining national confidence in our military programs.

The point was made earlier in this chapter that in three and a half years, the Joint Chiefs of Staff split formally on only twenty-three papers. It may be of interest to consider how these splits were handled and whose cause prevailed in the end.

Once the Joint Chiefs of Staff reach an impasse on an issue and determine that a further reconciliation of views is impossible, they instruct the Director of the Joint Staff to prepare a split paper for submission to the Secretary of Defense. This document contains an agreed statement of the conflicting views for easy comparison by the Secretary.

The position of the Chairman in these matters is somewhat different from that of the Chiefs. Until the reorganization of the Department of Defense in 1958, the Chairman was without the right of vote in the JCS deliberations. However, this disability was not a real one. The Chiefs do not engage in formal balloting; rather they submit divergent views to the Secretary of Defense when not in accord. The Chairman has always had the same ability to convey his views to the Secretary, doing so either orally or through a personal memorandum attached to the split paper. Admiral Radford established this latter practice, which was confirmed in the Department of Defense Reorganization Act of 1958, which gave the Chairman equal voting rights with the other Chiefs. The impression in Congress and among the public was that this action was a significant upgrading of the Chairman. Actually, it changed nothing of importance. Without a formal right to vote, the Chairman had already achieved a predominant position, overshadowing the Chiefs singly or in combination.

The primacy of the Chairman is clearly shown by the following box score setting forth the decisions of the Secretary of Defense on the twenty-three splits mentioned above. The breakdown shows how many times the Secretary supported or rejected the views of the services and the Chairman in these twenty-three splits covering most of the period 1955-1959.

	Supported	*Rejected*
Army	3	20
Navy	13	10
Marine Corps (participated in only 11 splits)	4	7
Air Force	17	6
Chairman (participated in only 21 splits)	18	3

To understand the relationships underlying this tabulation, certain additional facts should be pointed out. The Army, normally in a minority position, was supported only once by the Chairman in these 23 issues. The Air Force supported the Army 4 times, the Navy 10 times, while the Marines in 11 splits were with the Army 6 times. Most of the Navy-Marine support came to the Army after Admiral Radford's departure as Chairman.

The record shows that, in the period under consideration, the Chairman has normally supported the cause of his service of origin. Admiral Radford was with the Navy 10 out of 13 times. General Twining, taking part in 8 splits, supported the Air Force 8 times. The record also indicates that the presence of the Marines at the table normally gives the Navy two votes. In 11 splits, the Marines were with the Navy 9 times.

It is often stated that the Chiefs have an obligation to achieve unanimity if only to relieve the Secretary of Defense from making difficult military decisions (a statement with which I disagree). The record shows that on four occasions in this period the Secretary decided against the unanimous recommendation of the JCS—apparently unanimity among the Chiefs would not solve everything.

In general, what may be concluded from a study of these statistics? First, it is apparent that the Army has been in an isolated, minority position for the last four years. Actually, this period of Babylonian captivity should be extended back two more years to cover General Ridgway's tenure as Chief of Staff.

Initially, under Admiral Radford, the Army was pitted against the Chairman and usually the other Chiefs as well. This isolation gradually diminished somewhat as the Navy and Marines inclined to the support of the strategy of Flexible Response and the importance of limited war. But the point remains that during the past four years either the Army Chief of Staff has had an unusual gift for choosing the wrong side of the arguments or there has been a steam-rollering of a dissenting view worthy of the best traditions of Tammany Hall.

Another principal conclusion is that the Chairman's side nearly always wins. This fact is not surprising since he is the personal choice of the Secretary of Defense, with whom he is in close physical and spiritual rapport. The two men live side by side in the Pentagon. The Chairman accompanies the Secretary to many important meetings at home and abroad, where he serves as his principal military adviser. The Chairman soon becomes identified in the mind of the Secretary, and indeed elsewhere in and out of the government, as the authentic voice of the armed services. It is not uncommon to confuse the views of the Chairman with those of the corporate body of the Chiefs and to attribute mistakenly to the Chiefs the personal position of the Chairman. Such circumstances account for the primacy of the Chairman and probably make it inevitable. Certainly, it is important to the Secretary of Defense that the Chairman retain this predominant position.

A Secretary of Defense needs a strong Chairman to direct the work of the Chiefs, to keep their noses to the grindstone, and to extract from them timely advice and recommendations—preferably of a kind which can be accepted and approved without embarrassment. Advice can be unpalatable and unwelcome, particularly if it runs afoul of political or economic considerations which the Administration holds in great store. A Secretary will look to the Chairman to prevent this kind of advice and to bring forth harmonious views on appropriate subjects which can then be used in support of the Department's programs. If the Chairman is to perform this function, obviously the Secretary must back him on the split issues. The record shows that the Secretary has rarely failed the Chairman in the last four years.

Thus, the Chairman has come to be a sort of party whip, charged with conveying the official line to the Chiefs in the hope and expectation that they will be guided thereby in their actions. This was not so under General Bradley, who, as the first Chairman, maintained a position of meticulous neutrality in monitoring the discussions of the Chiefs. Admiral Radford was an able and ruthless partisan, who did his utmost to impose his views upon the Chiefs. For the two years during which I sat with the Chiefs under him, I rarely engaged in a serious discussion with my other colleagues. The debate usually became a heated dialogue between the Chairman and me in which neither succeeded in persuading the other. But regardless of my disagreements with Admiral Radford, I always had a grudging admiration for his singleness of purpose and his undeniable effectiveness in driving through the programs of the New Look.

General Twining, as Chairman, has taken a position somewhat between that of General Bradley and of Admiral Radford. He has been much less a partisan of the official line than Admiral Radford but, as a long-time advocate of Massive Retaliation, his decisive vote has always favored the Air Force and opposed a thorough strategic reappraisal.

After an examination of the foregoing evidence, it is not an overstatement to say that the Chairman of the Joint Chiefs of Staff has come to assume much of the power of the dreaded single Chief of Staff who has been the bugbear of the Congress and of some elements of the public in past discussions of defense organization. This power is not bad in itself, but it is concealed power unaccompanied by public responsibility—which *is* bad. Nor does he enjoy the full advantages which legally centralized authority would have in effecting rapid decisions and in expediting the conduct of business. The Chairman must still observe the procedures of consultation and debate with the other Chiefs, even though in the end he can impose his view. This camouflaged status of the Chairman should be taken into serious account in any consideration of future changes in the structure and organization of the Department of Defense.

No discussion of the role of the Joint Chiefs of Staff would be complete without some reference to their relation with the Congress. Unlike the practice in most countries with a parliamentary form of government, the Chiefs of Staff of the U.S. armed services, both in their service and their Joint Chief capacity, are required to appear frequently and testify before the committees of Congress. At a minimum there is an annual appearance before four committees, the Armed Services Committees of the House and Senate as well as the Appropriations Committees of both houses. In normal years there are other appearances on special subjects such as atomic energy, guided missiles, military manpower, the reserve components, and the military aid programs. The hearings on the defense budget are usually the most difficult for the Chiefs, as they raise inevitably the issue of their divided responsibility toward the Executive and Legislative branches of the government.

The problem of the Chief of Staff appearing before a Congressional committee is to "tell the truth and shame the devil," while remaining loyal to the decisions of the President and the Secretary of Defense. This is not a simple ethic to apply in practice. The point of view which I hold is that the service Chief should present his views vigorously within the Department of Defense during the formulation of the budget or of any other measure of similar importance. Having made every effort to guide his civilian superiors in the direction which he believes right, the Chief of Staff must accept the decisions of the Secretary of his service, of the Secretary of Defense, and of the President as final and thereafter support them before Congress. The alternative is resignation. Such an attitude is entirely consistent with the military tradition in which an officer is reared. In the Army, as in the other services, the staff officer is honor-bound to set forth his views boldly and without reservation until his commanding general has made a decision. Thereafter his task is to support that decision and to make it work.

But the problem of a Chief of Staff in Washington is not that simple. In the military service, an officer is not hailed before an outside authority and there required to indicate the advice which he had originally given his commanding general and to explain his reasons therefore. This is the position of the Chief of Staff before a Congressional committee. No sooner has he read his prepared statement supporting the position of the Defense Department than he must face a battery of interrogators bent upon bringing forth his original views and contrasting them with the ultimate position of the Secretary of Defense and of the President. Very shortly a Chief of Staff will find himself in the position either of appearing to oppose his civilian superiors or of withholding facts from the Congress. Personally, I have found no way of coping with the situation other than by replying frankly to questions and letting the chips fall where they may.

It is hard to suggest a remedy for this situation, which is one no military man enjoys. One alternative would be to refuse to permit military officers to appear before Congress and leave the defense of military matters to the civilian secretaries. This is the solution followed in Great Britain and many European countries. I doubt that it will ever be accepted in the United States, where the Congress wants to hear the facts from military men who presumably are without political motivation.

A second alternative would be to take the position that the advice of the Chiefs of Staff to their civilian superiors is privileged and not to be revealed under Congressional interrogation. Thus far the Executive authority has not seen fit to raise the storm that such a stand would create.

Both of these alternatives would have the disadvantage of depriving Congress of responsible military advice needed to discharge its constitutional responsibilities toward the armed forces. Each year the matters of national security are becoming increasingly complicated and technical, yet the members of Congress must legislate wisely with respect to them. To whom can they turn other than to the Chiefs of Staff, who are responsible for our national defense? To deprive them of access to the views of the Chiefs of Staff would inevitably force them to seek irresponsible sources of advice, to the probable detriment of their legislative actions. May not the answer be to establish a legal relationship between the Joint Chiefs of Staff and the Congress, making the former the military advisers to the Congress in the same way that they are now advisers to the Secretary of Defense, the National Security Council, and the President? In reality, this is the relationship which has been developed under current practice.

CHAPTER VII

THE FAILURE OF
DECISION-MAKING:
HOW MILITARY STRATEGY IS
FORMULATED IN FACT

THE SECRETARY of Defense shares with the Joint Chiefs of Staff the responsibility for the way in which our strategy-making machinery operates in fact. It is true that the guidance provided the Department of Defense by the National Security Council has often been cloudy, but this defect need not be a fatal handicap. As I have said before, it is possible to find language in the "Basic National Security Policy" to support almost any military program. It is broad enough to allow the Department of Defense to draw up its own "National Military Program" (similar to the one produced by the Army in 1955), capable of providing clear and unambiguous guidance to the Joint Chiefs of Staff and to the military services. To produce such a document, however, it would first be necessary to decide some of the basic issues which have lain unresolved for years about the Department of Defense.

The split views of the Joint Chiefs of Staff are usually the target for most of the criticism directed at our defective strategy-making. Actually, these splits are in the main symptoms of an ailment, not the ailment itself. They are most often specific cases arising from more fundamental issues which lie in the background of the day-to-day divergencies of the Joint Chiefs. Until a Secretary of Defense requires the Chiefs to identify these basic divergencies and to present them to him for decision, it will never be possible to avoid splits or to rise above piecemeal action in putting the Defense house in order. Let me cite a few examples of basic issues which require special treatment before much progress can be made toward developing a useful "National Military Program."

The overriding issue which forms the backdrop for all debates on strategy is the conflict between the strategy of Massive Retaliation and that which I have called the strategy of Flexible Response. Since the former was adopted as orthodox official policy in 1953 and has been faithfully implemented in the succeeding defense budgets up to the present time, we have spent our dollars consistently to support it, although we have allowed language to appear in the "Basic National Security Policy" of the NSC which has encouraged its opponents to struggle against it. Thus far, no Secretary of Defense has been willing to denounce Flexible Response as a heresy and to excommunicate its supporters. The rival trumpeters have been allowed to play their conflicting notes. As a result, this fundamental schism continues to split the Joint Chiefs of Staff and provides the basic divergence for many of the conflicts within that body.

Closely related to this basic issue is the matter of reliance upon the use of atomic weapons. If the military are assured of their use in unambiguous terms, it is obvious that the military forces required will be different in size, organization, and equipment from those required if the employment of atomic weapons is uncertain. The services have never been given a clear-cut statement allowing them to plan with complete confidence on the use or limitations of use of atomic weapons. This doubt exists particularly in the case of limited war, where they are required to guess when their political leaders will decide that the use of atomic weapons will serve the national objectives. In the absence of clear guidance, the Air Force and, to a lesser extent, the Navy have virtually eliminated their capacity for prolonged effectiveness with conventional weapons, while the Army has endeavored to retain a so-called "either/or" capability.

We have already alluded to the debates over the definition of general and limited war. Behind these semantic exercises, there is a very definite issue—will the United States ever again fight a major war exclusively with conventional weapons? In particular, if we enter into armed conflict with the USSR, will we use atomic weapons at the outset and without restrictions or will we attempt to achieve our ends, initially at least, without resort to atomic weapons? While the JCS cannot decide these questions, which involve far more than purely military matters, they can and should make recommendations to set in motion the decision-making process which ends with the President.

Another set of basic issues which have to be decided concern the required size and composition of the so-called functional forces—the atomic retaliatory force, continental air defense, overseas deployments, limited-war forces, and the like. How much of these forces is enough? As early as 1955 I urged Mr. Wilson to require the Joint Chiefs of Staff to come up with practical yardsticks to tell us how much we should buy of these operational forces. Admiral Radford, Mr. Quarles, and others opposed such a procedure, arguing that these military matters cannot be submitted to scientific or engineering analysis. There are too many imponderables. These objections were accepted and to this day there are no approved goals for the size and composition of the functional forces. Thus the Department of Defense builds the defense structure of the nation without blueprints, design models, or agreed factors of safety. It will never be possible for the JCS to produce an agreed tabulation of the forces needed for our security without first settling the basic question of how much is enough in the various operational categories. These yardsticks of sufficiency are the building blocks necessary to provide a solid foundation for defense planning.

There is a special group of problems which plague the Joint Chiefs of Staff, relating to the technical feasibility of new weapons systems. The Joint Chiefs of Staff are often required to recommend to the Secretary of Defense years in advance of production the numbers and types of new weapons for eventual procurement by the services. Since the research and development of a new weapon is usually the work of a single military department, this department tends to become the sponsor and proponent of the weapon in any discussion of its future use. The Chiefs of the other services are just as likely to be skeptical of the claims made for the new weapon and to view with a jaundiced eye its potential requirement for defense funds. Thus, the Army and the Navy have been inclined to pour cold water on the Air Force Bomarc pilotless interceptor, and the Air Force and the Navy have been equally unenthusiastic over the future of the Army's Nike-Zeus antiballistic missile.

These attitudes are not the results purely of service prejudice or pride of authorship. It is difficult to sort out the exaggerated claims of the manufacturers of new weapons and to get at the facts with regard to them. No single Chief of Staff has the time or the ability to check all the claims made by their advocates. Nonetheless, he is obliged to take sides with regards to the future of the weapon and the degree of reliance to be placed upon it, often before it exists and always long before it is ready for production and use.

Here is an area where the Secretary of Defense should be better able to determine the technical merits of the case than the Joint Chiefs of Staff. The questions involved are largely scientific or engineering in nature, and lend themselves to consideration by civilian experts outside of the interested military services. The Secretary of Defense could help immeasurably if he took responsibility for determining the degree of technical reliance to be placed on new weapons systems. The Chiefs would then be left only to answer the appropriate military questions. For example, if the Secretary of Defense gave it as his opinion after consultation with impartial experts that the Bomarc missile or the Nike-Zeus antimissile missile was technically feasible and would meet its specifications by a certain date, it would not be difficult for the JCS to decide if the weapon was needed and, if so, the numbers required at specified times.

The over-all point is that it is possible for the Secretary of Defense to make the existing machinery work better than it has. For one thing, he can get much closer to the Chiefs than has either Secretary Wilson or Secretary McElroy. Only once in my experience did Mr. Wilson ever sit down with the Chiefs for an extended period to try to understand their difficulties. This was at the time of the meeting of the Chiefs in Puerto Rico in March, 1956. Although I suggested informal conferences with Mr. McElroy, beginning shortly after he came into office, he never gave the Chiefs any real opportunity as a body for serious discussion of basic issues. Both Secretaries apparently preferred to get the views of the Chiefs indirectly, either in formal documents or by word of mouth from the Deputy Secretary of Defense, Mr. Quarles, or from the Chairman, Admiral Radford or General Twining. Meanwhile, the President held aloof from the internal issues of the Chiefs, depending on the Secretary of Defense to adjust the differences. On several occasions the desirability of informal meetings with the Chiefs was raised with the President and he always seemed highly receptive. In discussing the matter with me in July, 1957, he gave a directive to his staff that such meetings be set up with the Chiefs on a bimonthly basis. For reasons which I never learned, the schedule was not put into effect.

If the basic issues cannot be resolved by less formal methods, the Secretary of Defense can always direct the Chiefs to draw up a statement of the issues in a form to facilitate his decision. After establishing his own position on fundamental issues, he can then overcome the vagueness of higher guidance by writing some clear, unambiguous prose of his own. Such an act of leadership would reinstate the intended procedures of strategy-making and give the JCS a sound base of departure for the discharge of their part of the business. This kind of leadership has not been forthcoming. Hence the determination of United States strategy has become a more or less incidental by-product of the administrative processes of the defense budget.

From the discussion of the vicissitudes of the New Look in Chapters III and IV, it must be apparent that the Secretary of Defense, through the use of budgetary guidelines, has become the true artisan of our military strategy without necessarily foreseeing the end product. This setting of guidelines has not been an arbitrary action on his part, but one to which he has been impelled in carrying out the policies of the Executive branch of the government, especially the directives of the Bureau of the Budget. In the breakdown of the strategy-making machinery, he has felt obliged to get on with the business by establishing ground rules for budget formulation consistent with the expenditure targets of the Treasury. These ground rules have had the effect of shaping the military posture of the United States as it is today and as it will remain for years to come.

The guidelines employed have usually placed limitations on military manpower, on over-all defense expenditures, and frequently on the internal distribution of the expenditures between the services. At times there have also been limitations on the reserves of equipment, supplies, and ammunition which the services are allowed to accumulate to meet the needs of war. The trend each year has been to cut back upon the authorized war reserves and hence to diminish the length of time during which our forces can be supported in combat prior to receiving the expanded output of full-scale war production.

Once each service has received the budget guidelines, it then proceeds to develop its own service budget in consonance with them. As the work progresses, the Service Secretary and his Chief of Staff are frequently called before the Secretary of Defense and the Defense Comptroller to discuss the development of their budget. I always found

Mr. Wilson and Mr. McElroy most anxious to give each service its day in court and to receive a thorough briefing upon the effects of the budget guidelines on that service. But although these sessions generate a tremendous amount of discussion, I have never seen any evidence to suggest that they influence much the ultimate outcome. Regardless of the eloquence expended by the service representatives, as we have seen, the fixed percentage allocations of the budget have remained the same for years—Army 23 per cent, Navy and Marines 28 per cent, Air Force 46 per cent.

This method of budget-making by service has the serious defect of obscuring the impact of the budget upon the functional categories of the forces. In other words, the three services develop their forces more or less in isolation from each other, so that a force category such as the strategic retaliatory force, which consists of contributions of both the Navy and the Air Force, is never viewed in the aggregate. Similarly, it is impossible to tell exactly how much continental air defense is being obtained from the defense budget since this is another category to which several services contribute. In other words, we look at our forces horizontally when we think of combat functions but we view them vertically in developing the defense budget. President Eisenhower has well said, "The waging of war by separate ground, sea, and air forces is gone forever." This statement means to me that we should organize our fighting forces on the task force principle, allocating a proper balance of Army, Navy, and Air forces to the field commanders in consonance with the tasks to be accomplished. It is an anomaly that while thus thinking in terms of aggregate forces balanced for combat, we still "buy" our forces, so to speak, in terms of the Army, Navy, and the Air Force. As a result, no one really knows what the United States is getting for its money in terms of combat power from any single budget or from any series of budgets in combination.

Faced with the problem of explaining the defects of our present "vertical" budget-making, I concocted "The Parable of the Unhappy Mess Sergeant" and presented it to the National Press Club on June 25, 1959. It may be worth repeating here to illustrate this rather technical point.

Once upon a time there was a company commander who was having trouble with his company mess. The men complained about the food, the AWOL rate was high, and all the morale indicators were low. So, he decided to make a personal investigation.

It is to be noted that he did not call in any outside experts. He didn't feel the need of a dietitian or a hotel manager. He properly felt that outside advice without responsibility would be a doubtful help—in fact, he was an old-fashioned, vanishing, do-it-yourself type.

It didn't take the captain long to find out what the trouble was. It was the way in which his mess sergeant was running the kitchen. Now the mess sergeant was a fine, upstanding soldier, but he hadn't had much experience in running a mess. In fact, he had been chosen quite recently because of an outstanding record in the Finance Department.

Not being a specialist in running messes, the sergeant had to depend pretty much upon his four cooks and that is where much of the trouble lay. These cooks were four ornery, independent types with ideas of their own. As they liked to keep an eye on each other, they insisted upon being on the shift together all the time—they never took turns. Furthermore, while one was a little older than the rest, no single one of them was boss.

To complicate matters further, these cooks were all artists in their own right. Two of them had been trained together and liked to cook pretty much the same things. They went in for airy soufflés, *vol-au-vents* and that kind of thing. The third was a specialist in seafoods—what the French chefs call "the fruits of the sea." The fourth was a plodding, meat-and-potatoes fellow. They were all good in their own way, but the trouble was that they could never agree on the day's menu, so each one made up his own.

As a result, when it was time for the mess sergeant to leave in the morning to do the marketing, all four cooks would bring forward their different menus for the day, and urge their particular one on the harassed sergeant. As it was always late, the best the sergeant could do was to gather up all the lists and hurry off to market. He did note, however, that the money value of each list was about all he had to spend for the entire day.

So, at market he always had a bad time. There were loud vendors on all sides, hawking their wares and urging him to buy. So, he would purchase here and there what looked or sounded good, first verifying that at least one of his cooks had asked for it. When his money ran out he would go back to the company and turn his groceries over to the cooks, whom he always found in a bad humor and unhappy over his morning's work. And well they should be, because, try as they might, they were never able to produce from his shopping three reasonably balanced meals capable of satisfying the growing appetite of the company.

Well, it didn't take the captain long to decide that all this wasn't good. He rounded up the mess sergeant and the cooks and had a heart-to-heart talk. "Men," he said, "we're going to change all this. Sergeant, the first thing for you to do is to get a master menu from these cooks which is good for at least a week in advance, and then clear it with me. If these cooks don't work together, put the best one in charge and fire the rest. Now, it is important to stay within your ration allowance, but the main thing is to see that your meals are balanced and meet the nutrition standards. Don't be sold a bill of goods by those vendors in the market. Buy exactly what is called for by the master menu, and then see that the cooks turn out the chow in accordance with it. If you need any additional help in improving the mess, you might set up a mess council of a few of the oldest noncoms and ask them from time to time how they think the mess is doing."

All this was done. The mess soon improved and the AWOL's returned for duty. There were no longer complaints about too many desserts and not enough bread and meat. Breakfast was served in the morning and not at noon or at night. The morale went up, the mess sergeant kept his job, and the captain was promoted.

And why all this success? Because the captain had made a reappraisal of the situation in light of changed conditions and had adopted a method whereby each meal was a balanced aggregate to which each cook contributed, according to his skill and according to the needs of the men. Menu-making had become a single horizontal operation rather than several vertical operations conducted by the rival artists. The resulting harmony in the company was deafening.

Thus ends "The Parable of the Unhappy Mess Sergeant."

If the President is regarded as the captain, the Secretary of Defense as the unhappy mess sergeant and the cooks as the Chairman and three Chiefs of Staff, the suggestions of reform in defense procedures become obvious.

Under current practice, when the three services have cleared their individual budgets with the Secretary of Defense, he then puts all three together and adds the percentage reserved for the use of the Department of Defense. Although the Joint Chiefs of Staff participate as service Chiefs in the development of their own departmental budgets, up to this point, the Joint Chiefs of Staff as a body take no part in the formulation of the over-all budget.

It was at this point in 1959 that the Secretary of Defense suddenly tossed the 1960 budget to the Chiefs and asked their opinion as to its adequacy. This incident, recounted in Chapter IV, reflected a sudden realization on the part of the Secretary that he needed the endorsement of the Chiefs before sending his budget to the Congress. The public furor which later arose out of this event has caused a reconsideration of the appropriate role to be assigned to the Joint Chiefs in budget-making. Until this role is determined, there is a serious gap in the present procedure, which provides for no formal way of relating military requirements, programs, and budgets. The interlocking of these three factors is accomplished within each department with respect to its own service budget but there is no adequate procedure to perform this function of correlation at the Department of Defense level. As a consequence, our military strategy today is a result of administrative and budgetary happenstance rather than of an analytical appraisal of our military requirements and of a scientific budget formulation directed at supporting these requirements with all the resources available for national defense. Each year our existing military programs are projected forward by one more budgetary increment, following the same direction given it by budgetary actions of years before. In the language of the missile makers, the programs proceed by "inertial guidance," with little or no "command control" to reorient them to changed world conditions. Not only are these military programs ponderous and hence difficult to redirect, but there are powerful service and economic forces committed to the maintenance of their *status quo*. I feel sure that the continued emphasis on Massive Retaliation and on the requirements of general war arises as much from the practical difficulties of overcoming this inertial momentum and of resisting these external forces as from any real conviction as to the rightness of the orthodox strategy. The maintenance of the rigid percentage distribution by service of the budgets since 1953 is clear proof of the absence of flexibility in our military preparations. This frozen pattern could only be justified if the world had stood still since 1953 and I doubt that anyone would say that it has. While there may be disagreement as to what change should have been effected in these years, it is difficult to believe that this absence of change can be right.

CHAPTER VIII

FLEXIBLE RESPONSE—A NEW NATIONAL MILITARY PROGRAM

Now THAT we have identified some of the principal defects in our procedures for developing military strategy and employing our military resources, it becomes time to decide in a constructive way what to do about it. But first I would like to return to an assertion which has been made in the foregoing discussion to the effect that new factors have arisen which require a complete reappraisal of our military needs. Specifically, what are these factors and what is their bearing upon our security?

The first factor is the loss by the United States of technological superiority over the USSR in many fields of military weaponry. While it is dangerous to generalize on limited evidence, it is impossible to deny that the Soviet Union leads the United States today in such important areas as long-range missiles and certain aspects of operations in space. Having a well-developed skepticism toward information tending to inflate the strength of an enemy, I have been slow to accept the reality and the significance of the so-called Missile Gap. Reluctantly, I have concluded that there is indeed such a gap which, in combination with other factors which will be mentioned, has a most significant bearing upon our military security.

We have ample evidence that the Soviet Union went into high gear in the development of medium- and long-range missiles well before the United States. They saved their money on bombers and spent it on missiles. Also, we must accept the fact that they have been successful in their missile programs despite the occasional failures which all missile makers know so well. My personal conclusion is that until about 1964 the United States is likely to be at a significant disadvantage against the Russians in terms of numbers and effectiveness of long-range missiles—*unless heroic measures are taken now.*

This preponderant missile strength on the part of the Russians will be all the more significant because the United States will not have an effective antimissile defense during all or most of the period of the missile gap. As I've said, the Army foresaw the need for an antimissile missile shortly after World War II and in 1955, after numerous preliminary studies, initiated serious work on the Nike-Zeus antiballistic missile. This weapon is the only one under development which offers a present hope of coping with hostile ballistic missiles. In 1957, along with other representatives of the Army, I urged a crash $6-billion program in order to achieve an operational capability with the Nike-Zeus by 1961. The Secretary of Defense and my colleagues on the Joint Chiefs of Staff consistently opposed this program, alleging the uncertainty of its success. As a result of this opposition, there has been no major expenditure of funds on the Nike-Zeus except for research and development. Thus it appears impossible to expect an active antimissile defense for the United States for years—*unless heroic measures are taken now.*

These two new factors, the superior Soviet missile force and the nonexistent ballistic missile defense of the United States, combine to put our country in a very dangerous position in the mid-term future. Our present deterrent capability to prevent general atomic war rests upon our superiority in manned bombers, supplemented to a limited degree by guided missiles. The number of atomic delivery vehicles, available to us and our allies against Soviet targets, is today overwhelming; indeed I have called it excessive. However, our superiority in manned aircraft is a dwindling asset. Already we have evidence of strong Soviet surface-to-air missile defenses about some of the principal Soviet targets. If their air defense missiles are as good as ours and their numbers continue to increase, very shortly our bombers will have to pay a prohibitive price of admission to attack them.

By 1961 the Soviets should have a very significant ballistic missile force which will enjoy great advantages in the attack and pose serious difficulties to our retaliatory strikes. It may be anticipated that the Soviet missiles will be very difficult, if not impossible, to find. Airfields appear readily upon air photographs and make excellent targets for pre-planned strikes, but missile sites need have none of this conspicuousness. From what we know of the Soviet methods, we can count upon their taking full advantage of concealment, dispersion, and mobility for their missiles. Under such conditions, it will become impossible for our U.S. bombers and missiles to eliminate the Soviet missile threat even by an anticipatory strike. Thus, a target system based upon attacking the Soviet missile forces will offer little advantage during most of this time frame. Our security against general atomic war can rest only upon deterrence; there will be no purely military solution capable of eliminating the danger.

Likewise, the difficulty of absorbing a surprise blow from the Soviets also becomes enormously greater. The warning against incoming missiles will be a matter of minutes rather than of hours. As long as the United States is dependent largely upon manned bombers, the latter will be highly vulnerable to surprise strikes upon the easily located airfields. A surprise attack by ballistic missiles might well be followed up by manned bombers possibly using low-level attack techniques. In such a disaster, our civilian population would suffer catastrophic losses, particularly from fall-out, for which there has been no protection afforded on a nation-wide scale.

In summary, between now and 1961, because of our superiority in manned bombers which still have a reasonable chance of getting to target, the United States would appear to have a considerable advantage if not caught by surprise. If the USSR achieved a surprise blow, the survival probability on both sides would seem about even because the lesser number of Soviet delivery means would be largely offset by the inadequate protection of military and civil targets in the United States.

In the mid-term period beginning about 1961, the United States retaliatory force will include a mix of ballistic missiles and bombers operating from known, fixed sites in the United States. In limited compensation for this exposure of the retaliatory force, we can count upon having taken some dispersion and hardening measures and, if all goes well, upon having some operational Polaris missile submarines. But there can still be no antimissile defense (to include early warning) for several more years. The anti-bomber defense may be improved slightly but the low-level defense will be a question mark, as will any effective fall-out protection for the civil population.

In this period the USSR may be expected to have a marked superiority in ICBM's, in strategic target intelligence, and in the protection and concealment of its strategic strike forces. It will probably have a good antibomber defense and an advanced civil defense program. Under these conditions, the United States will be at a serious disadvantage in general atomic war regardless of how the first blow is struck. There are, however, ways to mitigate this disadvantage—*if heroic measures are taken now.*

The net effect for the present and mid-term future of the two foregoing factors will be a serious decline in the effectiveness of our deterrent capability for the prevention of general atomic war.

Up to now we have been justified in feeling that the likelihood of a deliberately planned initiation of general atomic war by either side of the power bloc appears highly unlikely. It has often been said that since the advent of megaton atomic weapons, the most probable form of military operations will be limited war, and history thus far supports that point of view. However, in the midrange future we have seen that our protection against deliberately initiated general atomic war will tend to decline. Under the changing conditions, the USSR might feel a considerably greater temptation to resort to a surprise attack, to which they might in the end succumb.

At the same time, the possibility of general war by mistake or miscalculation is constantly growing. The number of atomic weapons and atomic warheads in the hands of the opposing power blocs increases numerically each year, thereby enhancing the mathematical probability of disastrous accidents which might be misinterpreted as hostile acts. Thus, a third factor, growing out of the first two, must enter into our calculations. We can no longer rely with reasonable confidence upon our ability to deter general war but must make the indispensable preparations to assure survival in an atomic war initiated deliberately by the Soviets or growing out of mistake or accident.

This decline in deterrent capability is serious not only in relation to our exposure to possible defeat in general war but also in increasing our vulnerability to atomic blackmail and attrition-type aggressions in many quarters of the world. For years it has been predicted that in a period of mutual deterrence the Soviets would indulge in a rising level of provocations. In 1959, we are in such a period and many episodes have verified the prediction. The Communist tactics in relation to Taiwan, the Middle East, Berlin, and Laos provide examples of the growing use of military power to support an aggressive course of action under the conditions of cold or limited war. As the Soviets become more assured of their superiority in general-war weapons, particularly in intercontinental ballistic missiles, and if they sense American timidity, they may be expected to press harder than ever before, counting upon submissiveness arising from our consciousness of weakness. They will not believe, nor will our friends, that we will use our massive retaliatory forces for any purpose other than our own survival. How then are we to meet the anticipated Communist provocations of the future?

These considerations lead to an evaluation of the fourth new factor, our inferiority to the Communist bloc in conventional forces. This condition is the result of a deliberate decision by our leaders to accept this inferiority, hoping to offset it by the threat of Massive Retaliation.

Since our disastrous demobilization in 1945, the Soviet advantage on the ground has steadily increased, except perhaps briefly during the Korean emergency. During recent years the Soviets have maintained an army of some two and a half million men, which they have completely re-equipped since World War II with the most modern conventional and atomic weapons. This army, more than the Soviet ballistic missiles, is the symbol of ruthless Communist power and a political weapon of tremendous value to the USSR. Under the New Look strategy, the United States has sought to convince the world that we could offset these conventional ground forces by threatening to blast them from the earth with atomic bombing if they committed aggression against us or our friends. Now our growing inferiority in effective general-war weapons nullifies whatever intrinsic worth this threat of Massive Retaliation ever had. Yet in spite of these facts, there are still voices to assert the impossibility of having a limited war in the NATO area. Such an assertion means that any collision of patrols over, say, Berlin would automatically result in general atomic war. It offers no alternative other than reciprocal suicide or retreat in the face of the superiority of Soviet conventional forces. Such talk does little to reassure our allies in Europe. Furthermore, it is nonsense. If men who are both sane and determined continue to direct nations, they will initially take all measures short of general war to resist aggression—regardless of the nationality of the aggressor.

Why has the United States made no determined effort to develop conventional forces comparable to those of the

USSR? For one thing, we have accustomed ourselves to saying, and perhaps to believing, that we are hopelessly outnumbered by the Communist bloc. This statement as a generalization is simply not true. The following tabulation shows a current estimate of the men of military age in the Communist and in the Free World areas:

COMPARATIVE MANPOWER IN FIT MALES OF MILITARY AGE

Free World (In Millions)			Communist Bloc (In Millions)		
U. S.	31.0		USSR	41.0	
NATO (less U. S.)	54.4		European Satellites	17.4	
		85.4			58.4
SEATO (less U. S., U. K., and France)	20.4		Chinese Communists	84.5	
Organization of American States (Less U.S.)	24.0		North Korea	.9	
			North Vietnam	1.6	
Iran	2.2		Total	145.4	
Republic of Korea	2.8				
Japan	18.3				
Chinese Nationalists	2.4				
South Vietnam	1.4				
Total	156.9				

The fact is that the Free World has preponderant manpower in all strategic areas except the Far East, and there much of the Communist Chinese manpower is unusable because of logistic limitations. The Free World can defend itself solely by the force of conventional weapons if its leaders are willing to pay the price. Fortunately, the lead time of preparation required to reverse the present unfavorable balance of conventional strength does not exceed two to three years. Thus, we could do something about the present situation in a much shorter time than we could change the balance in long-range missiles and antimissile defenses, where the lead time of research, development, and production is much greater. *But the time for decision is now.*

In summary, the United States faces a period of several years in which we will be inferior to the USSR both in general-war and in conventional, counterattrition forces. It will be a period in which our leaders will be hard put to maintain our world position in the face of the probable increased Soviet pressures. These adverse conditions will tend to loosen the bonds of our alliances and to increase the trend toward neutralism and compromise among the weak. The haunting fear of general atomic war through Soviet surprise attack or through miscalculation will bear heavily upon our leaders, faced with the requirement to act decisively under these conditions of inferiority. This critical disability of our country and of the Free World can be offset and corrected only by the adoption at once of a few "quick fixes," which will cost relatively little in time and money. Concurrently, we should recast our longer-term efforts in a National Military Program of Flexible Response.

The "quick fixes" are four in number:

1. Improved planning and training for limited war.
2. Exploitation of the mobile Intermediate Range Ballistic Missile (IRBM).
3. Better protection for the Strategic Air Command.
4. A limited fall-out shelter program.

The last two points need little comment. Our manned bombers on airfields known to the enemy are becoming increasingly vulnerable to surprise attack. Since we must still depend upon them for several years to come and since the "hardening" of bases (i.e., protection by covering with concrete or by burying important installations) is so expensive, the best we can do is to disperse the bombers over more airfields and keep the maximum feasible number on air alert.

The reasonably complete protection against atomic attack on centers of governmental controls and of civil population is a gigantic undertaking of great expense. However, every study of population casualties in an atomic exchange indicates the great advantage of very simple shelters which protect only against fall-out. The cost of such a national program would not be excessively high and the protection achieved would fully warrant its inclusion as a relatively "quick fix."

The need to exploit the mobile IRBM requires some explanation. The Army has always felt that a mobile intermediate-range ballistic missile offers great possibilities as a reinforcement to our atomic deterrent forces. With this objective in mind, since November, 1955, it has pushed the development of the Jupiter IRBM under the able leadership of Major General John B. Medaris, Dr. Wernher von Braun, and his team of German-American scientists. However, this project received a serious setback in November, 1956, when Secretary Wilson made the fatal decision to give the operational control of the Jupiter to the Air Force. This decision amounted virtually to killing the program, because this Army-built weapon has never appealed to the Air Force.

In particular, the Air Force was opposed to giving mobility to the IRBM. Although the Jupiter was specifically designed for field mobility, in November, 1958, the Air Staff directed the Army to remove this feature completely as if it were something unholy. The reason for this attitude is hard to determine. Perhaps it is the fact that the Air Force is accustomed to think in terms of airfields with acres of concrete and permanent buildings. Perhaps it is also the fact that a mobile missile needs Army-type troops to move, emplace, protect, and fire it. Such troops include transportation units for mobility on the road and across country, engineer troops for road and site construction, signal troops for field communications, infantry for close defense, and ordnance units for repair and maintenance. All these would be needed if the Jupiter were used in its mobile configuration. Thus, a decision to organize mobile ballistic missile units would in logic have led to transferring the operational use of the weapon back to the Army—where it should have been all the time.

Whatever the causes for the situation, the IRBM is not giving the United States a return on the vast sums of money expended on it. With the U.S. Air Force cool to its employment by U.S. units, the government has endeavored to interest our allies in IRBM units. This project has encountered so many political difficulties that at the present time only the United Kingdom has accepted an IRBM (the Thor). While other factors are present in this foreign reluctance, the fact that these missiles are fixed and without mobility is a reminder to a recipient country that they would be stationary bull's-eyes upon home territory, which would invite atomic attack in case of general war. Meanwhile, the Jupiter missile has been carefully tested and developed into a weapon of great accuracy and of high potential value. Its mobility can be restored. Yet it remains a sterile asset at a time when the United States faces the consequences of the ICBM missile gap.

Consequently, in my opinion, one of the "quick fixes" which we should adopt at once is a revival of the Jupiter IRBM program, its allocation to the Army as a mobile field weapon and the rapid deployment of units overseas into areas within range of important Soviet targets. I would see no obstacles to their deployment to territory under United States control, and many of the difficulties in obtaining acceptance in foreign countries would disappear if the weapon could be moved into the mountains, valleys, and deserts, using railroad trains, trucks, and barges to give it mobility.

The first "quick fix" on the list above is designed to get the most out of the limited-war forces which we have. These are found generally in the Continental United States and consist of a composite of Army, Navy, Marine, and Air Force units entirely unrelated to each other in planning and training.

There are no approved joint plans on the books of the JCS for the assembling, training, and rapid outloading of these heterogeneous forces, which represent our principal resources, to reinforce our overseas garrisons or to cope with the brush fires of limited war. There is no single headquarters anywhere which supervises the planning for overseas movements or which verifies readiness for movement. While joint training exercises involving some of these units do occur from time to time, they are conducted irregularly and generally with restricted funds. I would favor establishing a joint headquarters similar to the Strategic Air Force, to be charged with the joint planning, training, and transport of all forces of all services earmarked for possible use in limited war. Such a headquarters would have the same dedication to readiness for limited war as is shown by the Strategic Air Force in preparation for general war. The cost would be negligible, but the advantage gained very considerable.

In order to plan for the rapid movement of its forces, this Limited War Headquarters should have some idea of the strategic air and sea lift available. This is a particularly vital question for the Army units, since by the nature of its organization, the Army is a hitchhiker on the Air Force and the Navy and must look to these services for provisions of strategic lift. Thus far, no prior allocation for planning purposes has been made to the Army of the aircraft and ships necessary to move any of its units. When the Army inquires who will give it a ride, the answer is that the Joint

Chiefs of Staff in an emergency will decide the matter. Thus, no advance planning is possible between the Army, the Air Force, and the Navy for the purpose of reducing the reaction time of spearhead forces ordered to an overseas destination.

Since it would be plainly uneconomical to tie down aircraft on airfields while they awaited a possible Army mission, I have never suggested any such action nor, I believe, has any other responsible Army spokesman. It would be most helpful, however, if the Air Force would predesignate certain squadrons of strategic air lift for joint planning with Army commanders. The airplanes of their units could go about their business in the United States unhampered by this requirement, but their commanders would know that in an emergency their units would immediately be ordered to certain airfields to move specific Army units. Thus the Army and Air Force commanders could work out detailed joint plans and assure the launching of an overseas movement with maximum celerity and efficiency. The Limited War Headquarters could hold checks and rehearsals to verify the readiness of these forces. The foregoing measures taken together would afford a cheap but important "quick fix" for our limited-war deficiencies.

Having got the "quick fixes" under way as a matter of urgency, we then have the more far-reaching task of national reappraisal of our strategy and its reorientation toward Flexible Response. It should take into account the new factors which make this appraisal necessary, evaluate their impact as well as the effect of the "quick fixes," and establish specific objectives for the new program. These objectives should be to deter nuclear attack on the United States, to deter or defeat limited aggression anywhere (including a Communist attack on NATO with conventional forces), and to make provision for essential survival measures in the unhappy event that general war is not deterred or comes through miscalculation.

At the outset of this reappraisal, we should recognize and accept the limitations of our atomic retaliatory forces. Under the conditions which we must anticipate in the coming years, it is incredible to ourselves, to our allies, and to our enemies that we would use such forces for any purpose other than to assure our national survival. When would our survival be at stake? Two clear cases would be an atomic attack on the Continental United States or the discovery of indisputable evidence that such an attack was about to take place. A third possible case would be a major attack upon Western Europe, since the loss of that area to Communism would ultimately endanger our national survival. These seem the only situations imaginable in which our atomic retaliatory forces might be deliberately used. Hence, they are the only situations to which their deterrence applies.

Having recognized the limitations of our atomic deterrent forces, we should, in consistence, redefine general war as being synonymous with a nuclear exchange between the United States and the USSR. Limited war would then be left to cover all other forms of military operations. The question of using atomic weapons in limited wars would be met by accepting the fact that primary dependence must be placed on conventional weapons while retaining readiness to use tactical atomic weapons in the comparatively rare cases where their use would be to our national interest.

The National Military Program of Flexible Response should contain at the outset an unqualified renunciation of reliance on the strategy of Massive Retaliation. It should be made clear that the United States will prepare itself to respond anywhere, any time, with weapons and forces appropriate to the situation. Thus, we would restore to warfare its historic justification as a means to create a better world upon the successful conclusion of hostilities.

These broad, fundamental decisions as to the objectives and nature of our strategy, the use of atomic weapons, and the definitions which indicate the kinds of war which we must prepare to fight should be taken by the President on the recommendation of the National Security Council. When approved, they would serve as the basis for action by the Joint Chiefs of Staff in determining the type, size, and priority of the military forces required to execute the approved strategy.

In a field where costs are staggering, it is essential that our new Military Program put first things first and know why the priority is right. In my judgment, the first priority of our Military Program is a double-barreled extension of our "quick fixes"—to modernize and protect the atomic deterrent force and to build up our limited-war, counterattrition forces to offset the present preponderant Soviet forces on the ground. Thereafter, I would make carefully selective provision for continental air defense, for the requirements of full mobilization, and for survival measures to hedge against the failures of deterrence. Our money will go fast in these latter areas and it will not be clear how much we can do until the over-all program is costed in some detail.

Assuming that the Secretary of Defense approves this priority of effort in concept, the JCS would then be ready to get down to the brass tacks of determining the kinds and sizes of specific forces required and the way to use them— in the jargon of the Pentagon, to determine the criteria of sufficiency, the force tabs, and the strategic concept.

The statement of the strategic concept as it might be written into our Military Program would indicate how the United States expects to employ its military forces under conditions of cold, limited, and general atomic war. It would indicate broadly where the weight of our effort would lie and would assign general tasks to our forces at home and abroad in anticipation of various military contingencies.

A listing without regard to priorities of the kinds of forces necessary to implement this strategic concept would include: first, the atomic deterrent forces, both their offensive and defensive components; second, the continental air defense forces in the United States; third, our overseas deployments; fourth, strategic reserve forces in the United States;

fifth, the air and sea forces necessary to give strategic mobility to the U.S. reserves and to maintain the air and sea lines of communications. There will be no difficulty getting agreement among the Chiefs that we need some of all of these types. But the question of how much of each is a hard one, upon which we can expect them to divide. But if we are consistent with the priority effort which we adopted above, a solution should be possible, at least in qualitative terms.

There is no argument over a top priority for the modernization and protection of the atomic deterrent forces. We must provide for a striking force which is clearly capable of surviving a surprise attack and of inflicting unacceptable losses on the USSR. This means there must be an offensive and a defensive component. The size of the offensive part can be determined fairly accurately, figuring back from the enemy targets which, if destroyed, will represent the loss of his war-making capacity. These targets amount only to a few score, at the most to a few hundred. After due allowance has been made for aborts, enemy action, and failures both human and mechanical, the number of atomic vehicles needed to destroy this target system can be determined by simple arithmetic. Even after adding a heavy factor of safety to cover imponderables, the size of the required atomic retaliatory force will be found to be much smaller than the bombers and missiles of our present force.

The size of the force is only one part of the problem—the quality is even more important. Our Military Program must inject new life into the long-range missile program—

not the Atlas, Titan, Redstone, and Regulus, but their successors, the Minuteman of the Air Force, the Pershing of the Army and the Polaris of the Navy. For protection, all will need mobility, dispersion, and concealment, as well as early warning.

In addition to these passive, protective measures, the deterrent force must have an active, defensive component based largely on the Nike-Zeus antiballistic-missile missile. We need a crash program to make up for the time lost by past indecision. It is the only weapon in sight for the job and we cannot afford to be without it. Also we shall continue to need some bomber defense against both high- and low-flying bombers. The Zeus, though capable of coping with incoming missiles, is not designed to shoot down aircraft. The Nike-Hercules and Hawk will have this role to play for some years to come.

So much for the size, composition, and modernization of the atomic deterrent force. In equal priority is the need to improve what we have called limited-war or counterattrition forces. It is perhaps a mistake to label them limited-war forces because all of them have an important use in case of general war. These counterattrition forces have a dual capability for either limited or general war, whereas the strictly general-war forces do not have this flexibility. A B-52 bomber, an ICBM missile, or a Polaris submarine are good for use in general war and for little else. An Army division or a tactical air squadron has a use in any kind of war.

Under the National Military Program of Flexible Response, the JCS will need to increase significantly the attention paid heretofore to the counterattrition forces. Their required size can be determined by studies and war games of hypothetical military situations assumed to arise in various sensitive areas. These studies will show the rate at which our forces will need to arrive, the total number needed to restore peace, and the length of time required to do the job. These figures will then determine the size of the regular and reserve forces to be maintained in the U.S., and the quantities of supplies to be accumulated in war reserve. Such studies will indicate, I believe, the need for an extensive program to improve our capability for waging limited war.

In emphasizing this need, I would not suggest that we are without current assets for this purpose. If one regards the force structure of our three services, one finds that nearly all of the Army and of the Marine Corps, much of the Tactical Air Force, some of the Navy's carriers, and large parts of our strategic air and sea lift may be accounted limited-war forces and available in an emergency. While this statement is accurate as far as it goes, it does not take into account our lack of planning and organization to make the most of these assets. For this reason, as Chief of Staff of the Army, I proposed a five-point program to improve the limited-war capability of all the services. It included the improvement in planning, training, and air movement previously included in the "quick fixes." In addition, this program called for the modernization of the organization and equipment of the limited-war forces of all three services. This modernization would give consideration to the characteristics of the geographical areas in which limited war is likely to occur, as well as the armaments of potential enemies and the military capabilities of indigenous allies. Bearing in mind that limited wars are not necessarily either small or short wars, the modernization program would take into account the needs of the first six months of war—both our own and those of our possible allies. With regard to atomic weapons, it would provide our forces with small tactical atomic weapons but they would remain prepared to fight entirely without them. Reversing the current emphasis, these forces would place main, but not sole, reliance upon conventional weapons. This change of attitude would have an important effect upon the design of future tactical bombers and aircraft carriers as well as upon the plans for supporting logistic systems on land. In the design of tactical atomic weapons, emphasis should be placed upon developing those of very low yield, which offer no hazards of fall-out nor serious danger to friendly troops and allied populations.

Another point in the program concerned itself with improving the strategic mobility of limited-war forces. Staff studies and war games of hypothetical, limited-war situations always develop logistic limitations and bottlenecks affecting adversely the movement of our forces. The size of our landing in Lebanon in July, 1958, was controlled by the capacity of the single airfield and port at Beirut. Similarly, military movements to other parts of the world will inevitably encounter limitations which can only be removed by prior identification and elimination. The prompt projection of naval power about the world is possible today only because the British and U.S. navies long ago determined the needs for harbors, port facilities, and fuel supplies at strategic world points and provided for the need in advance. A similar analysis of the future requirements for the mobility of limited-war forces is necessary on the part of the joint staffs of the United States and its allies. Improved mobility will also come from the modernization program, which should produce better ships and planes for strategic movement. The Army likes very much the roll-on-roll-off type of ship with which the Navy has been experimenting. New jet cargo land and sea planes offer great advantages for fast air movement. Our National Military Program must be prepared to make an annual allotment of funds for these measures for improved mobility.

If these two long-term projects, the modernization of counterattrition forces and the improvement of their mobility, are carried out along with the planned "quick fixes," we will then be prepared to proceed to the final point. By that time we will not merely talk a good game in terms of our limited-war capability, we will be prepared to play a good game as well. Under these conditions, it will be important to display our peacetime readiness to move limited-war forces anywhere about the globe. Periodic demonstrations of this sort would have a great political effect in that they would show our friends that we are capable of responding militarily with something other than a heavy atomic weapon. By the same token, we would show our enemies that we are prepared to resist attrition quickly and effectively. In conjunction with our atomic deterrent forces, we would have counterattrition forces capable of extending the scope of our potential military reaction across the entire spectrum of possible challenge in accordance with a strategy of Flexible Response.

Two categories of forces which fall into this double-barreled, first priority of effort deserve special attention. The first are our overseas deployments in Europe and the Far East. They have an important part to play both in deterring and in fighting general and limited war. In general war, they must cover the vital ground areas in which they are deployed and hold the enemy at arm's length while we punish him with our heavy weapons of great destruction. Thereafter they must have the residual strength to occupy his lands and claim whatever may be called the victory. For limited war, they must be strong enough to turn back infiltrations, raids, and border forays and gain the necessary time to make sure of an enemy's intentions. They should be able, if needed, to detach forces to adjacent areas in the way that our forces in Europe provided elements for the Lebanon landing.

Apart from their strictly military requirement, these overseas deployments have a very important psychological role to play. They exemplify to our allies the willingness of the United States to share with them the hazards of living under the Communist guns. There is no substitute for the personal sharing of the danger. I was in Berlin in 1950 at the time that our troops were sent into Korea to stop the Communist invasion. Interested in the German reaction, I asked a leading Socialist of Berlin what he thought of our action. For a man of his pacifistic and antimilitary leanings, I was surprised to find him highly in favor of the U.S. decision to act. When I asked why, he replied, "We Germans have always known you Americans are generous and kind-hearted. Look at what the Marshall aid has done for Berlin. But we never were sure how you really stood until you offered Korea the lives of your sons and not *pfannkuchen* [pancakes]."

Even the dependents accompanying our soldiers play a part in establishing the earnestness of our intentions. Again in Berlin, at a time when the Soviets were putting heavy political pressure on the town, I asked a citizen why the city remained so calm. "It will be time to worry when your family leaves," he replied.

So the National Military Program must continue to provide for overseas deployments certainly at no lower strength than at present. Actually, we have trimmed their personnel so often in recent years that a moderate increase is needed to balance the internal composition of these forces.

The other point needing special comment is the requirement in the top priority for a back-up of military strength in the form of strategic reserves in the U.S. This point has been touched on before but it needs to be emphasized. We must have a large bloc of mobile forces ready for quick intervention either to put out a brush fire, to reinforce our overseas garrisons, or to effect a prompt strengthening of our general military posture in a time of tension. Regular forces in being must be available for the immediate tasks in the first few months of an emergency, but thereafter we can call upon selected civilian reserve units which have been given particular attention in time of peace. These forces must have all the equipment, supplies, and munitions necessary for at least six months of combat. Thereafter expanded war production will begin to take over the burden. But this early back-up is so vital that it must be paid for in the first priority of our efforts.

Passing to second priority forces and activities, we must consider the scope to give to continental air defense beyond that proposed above to defend our retaliatory forces. This question is likely to remain as difficult a problem under the new Military Program as it has been in the past. It is hard to be sure of the right course of action because of the great cost of air-defense weapons and installations, their untested effectiveness in war, and the fact that they will never be used if our general-war deterrent succeeds. Nonetheless, it is apparent that some level of air defense is necessary, if only to maintain the morale of our citizens and to inject the greatest possible factor of doubt into the war plans of the Soviet General Staff. Such a defense should give preponderant attention to the growing ballistic missile threat, but for some time to come cannot ignore the dangers of high- and low-level bomber attack.

The quantity of air defense required is susceptible to a mathematical analysis, which is more or less the converse of the problem of determining the size of our atomic deterrent forces. It is possible to assume that the protection of certain percentages of our population and industrial capacity is necessary to assure survival in the case of general atomic war, then to site air-defense weapons and installations capable of giving a high mathematical probability of attaining that level of protection. However, the result will be no better than the initial assumption, which is exposed to a high degree of uncertainty since no one can really conceive of the effects of a massive atomic attack upon a modern nation. Nonetheless, no better way has occurred to anyone for establishing some scientific basis for air-defense sufficiency. The cost of any such program is likely to make it unfeasible at the optimum level, so that the task would be divided into two parts, that for protecting a limited number of vital areas and the remainder required for a fairly complete defense of our homeland. The first part should be supported in second priority behind the deterrent and counterattrition forces, the second at the end of our list among the hedges against the failure of deterrence.

Having determined the size and the quality of the atomic deterrent forces, the counterattrition forces, and the most important forms of continental air defense, the artisans of the new Military Program will reach the grab-bag category of forces needed to hedge against the failure of deterrence of general atomic war or of protracted conventional war.

There will be a competition for resources among the requirements of a total conventional mobilization, a higher level of continental air defense, more antisubmarine warfare forces, civil defense beyond the "quick fix" fall-out shelter program, stockpiling to offset bomb damage, and other expensive programs. Fiscal availability and common sense will be the only guidelines for the military planners. However, they will be consoled in the knowledge that up to this point our preparations have had a rational basis and that there is justified confidence in their over-all deterrent effect. With justified faith in deterrence, there will be less need for concern about hedges against its failure.

Thus far in the discussion of priorities and forces we have said little about antisubmarine warfare forces and where they fit in. They have always been difficult to classify with finality because many of the ships and airplanes involved in antisubmarine warfare are capable of other missions as well. An antisubmarine warfare aircraft carrier, for example, may provide air support to Army forces in limited war, as was often the case in Korea.

However, considering these forces only in their antisubmarine role, where do they fall in the priorities established under the National Military Program of Flexible Response? Naval forces engaged in the surveillance of the USSR submarine fleet and in protecting the shores of the United States from enemy missile-firing submarines would apparently fall into the first priority, as would those naval elements necessary to assure the freedom of the sea lanes for the movement of counterattrition forces. The remainder of the antisubmarine warfare forces, however, would fall largely in the third category, of hedges against the failure of the deterrence of general war. Only in the latter event will the Soviet submarines swarm out to sea and present a serious menace to the sea lanes. Incidentally, considering the size of the Russian U-boat fleet, their leaders are apparently not counting on the next war being a short one.

Another observation with regard to our antisubmarine warfare forces is that they are less likely to encounter obstacles in the use of atomic weapons than our ground and air forces. Since their objectives are identifiable military targets found in areas generally removed from civilian populations where the fall-out hazards are minimal, it would appear reasonable to count on the use of atomic weapons with fewer restrictions than ashore. This assurance is increased by the fact that action against enemy submarines is likely to occur only in the context of general war with the USSR.

To tabulate the conclusions of the foregoing discussion, the new Military Program should provide for the following forces and resources in the indicated order of priority.

PRIORITY I

KIND	SIZE AND COMPOSITION
1. Atomic deterrent forces a. Offensive retaliatory	A few hundred reliable and accurate missiles, supplemented by a decreasing number of bombers capable

	of destroying a sufficient number of vital Soviet targets to assure destruction of enemy war-making capability. To be mobile, concealed, and dispersed.
b. Active defensive	Enough Nike-Zeus, Nike-Hercules, and Hawk missile batteries to protect the offensive retaliatory forces. Sophisticated early-warning service capable of timely reporting of incoming missiles.
2. Counterattrition	Size to be based on studies of hypothetical limited wars. Modernized in weapons, equipment, air and sea lift. To carry very-small-yield atomic weapons but be prepared to fight with conventional weapons alone.
3. Overseas deployments	Generally, same unit composition as now, but modernized like the other counterattrition forces and

moderately increased in numerical size to achieve better internal balance.

4. Mobile reserve forces and supplies

A partial mobilization to assure a back-up of units, trained individuals, supplies, and equipment necessary to support at least the first six months of combat.

5. Air and sea lift to move and support the foregoing categories of forces

Progressively modernized through introduction of cargo jet land and sea planes and roll-on-roll-off shipping.

6. Antisubmarine warfare forces

Those necessary for surveillance of USSR submarine fleet and for defense of the atomic retaliatory force against missile-launching submarines.

PRIORITY II

1. Continental air defense

Emphasis on defense against missiles. Weapons comprise principally Nike-Zeus, Nike-Hercules, and

Hawk missiles. Size sufficient to give —— per cent probability of protection to —— per cent of U.S. population and industry. (JCS to determine percentages from specific studies.)

2. Antisubmarine warfare forces

Those necessary to protect foregoing U.S. targets from attack by submarine-launched missiles, especially civilian targets (if there is a requirement beyond forces in Priority 1-6 above).

PRIORITY III

1. Hedges against the failure of deterrence
   a. Requirements of general mobilization
   b. Remaining needs of air defense
   c. Civil defense
   d. Remaining needs for antisubmarine warfare
   e. Stockpiling against bomb damage

Size and character of these programs indeterminable. Depends largely on resources left over for these purposes after meeting requirements in higher priorities.

We have now said enough about the kinds and quantities of military forces required to support a National Military Program of Flexible Response. It is now time to consider how the defense budget should be constructed to assure that our defense dollars are spent in consistence with the foregoing priorities. Here are the steps, as I see them, which should be taken to build a budget on horizontal principles in support of the functional categories of forces above.

It is assumed that by this point in building our new program the Joint Chiefs of Staff have produced a strategic concept based on a strategy of Flexible Response and have agreed on the priorities of forces tabulated above. They have submitted this preliminary work to the Secretary of Defense, who has given it his approval. The Joint Chiefs of Staff should now determine the specific forces, in terms of units of the Army, Navy, Marines, and Air Force, which are necessary to fill out the approved functional categories according to the priorities. In so doing, they would first call upon the unified commanders overseas to submit their estimates of the kinds and quantities of forces which they require to perform their missions. The unscreened total of these overseas requirements will probably be excessive and the Joint Chiefs of Staff will have to amalgamate and modify them, taking into account overlaps and duplications unknown to the individual commanders. They would then present the refined force structure to the Secretary of Defense for his approval.

The Secretary of Defense will always be concerned about defense costs, as he will inevitably have been the recipient of Administration guidance from the Bureau of the Budget. Hence, he would now refer the recommended force structure to the Defense Comptroller and the military services for rough costing estimates. The Comptroller would supervise this work and would return the results to the Joint Chiefs of Staff, who by this time would have received from the Secretary of Defense an indication of the approximate over-all dollar ceiling for the defense budget.

The Chiefs would now have the difficult task of compressing the desired force structure within a dollar ceiling, which we hope would be a reasonable one, related in size to the enemy threat. To do this compression, they would need to consult repeatedly the overseas commanders as well as the military services. It would be most useful if they could present to the Secretary of Defense two or more force structures, corresponding to as many levels of fiscal availability. This device would permit the Secretary of Defense to see clearly the implications of fiscal limitations on the Armed Forces.

In the end, the Secretary of Defense must discharge his grave responsibility of making the decision—following discussions with the President—which will determine the military posture of the United States for the next three or four years. No one else can do it for him; it is an essential part of the job. But whatever his decision, if a procedure such as the one outlined herein has been followed, he will have successfully linked together military missions, force structure, and the budget, an accomplishment that has never yet been achieved.

CHAPTER IX

A NEW AND CERTAIN TRUMPET

AT THIS point the question may well be raised as to whether such a National Military Program of Flexible Response is really practicable. It is if we will act promptly. Changes must be made both within the Department of Defense and in the national attitude and behavior. To start with, the attic of the Department of Defense has need of a thorough housecleaning to throw out many outmoded concepts, illusions, shibboleths, and fallacies.

This housecleaning should start with a rewriting of the roles and missions of the three services. The present roles and missions were promulgated in 1947 at the time of the famous Key West conference and have not been changed in any significant way since then. In their initial form, their statement was little more than a description of the capabilities of the services at the time of the promulgation of the Key West Agreement. Since that time, weapons systems, tactics, and strategy have changed, and with them the capabilities of the services.

A new concept of the role of the services has arisen, which was the guiding thought of the reorganization of the Department of Defense in 1958. This reorganization removed the military departments from the channel of operational command and made their primary function one of organizing, equipping, and training forces having the distinguishing characteristics of the Army, Navy, and Air Force. For operations, these forces when ready for combat pass to the control of field commanders who, under the strategic direction of the Joint Chiefs of Staff, command them and integrate their actions. But the problem remains of redefining what we mean by Army, Navy, and Air Force. What are their distinguishing characteristics which make them different one from the other? What can one type of unit do that the other cannot which thus justifies its independent existence? To answer these pertinent questions requires a return to a consideration of fundamental roles and missions.

To produce a new statement of the roles and missions would require the painstaking collaboration of some of the best minds of all the military services. I will undertake only to outline the direction which I would favor for these efforts. The first requirement would be to redefine the three services in clear, simple language to show what they are and are not. I would define the Army, Navy, and Air Force in functional terms as those services within the Department of Defense charged respectively with providing the military forces necessary for the successful prosecution of sustained combat operations in a land, sea, and air environment. (I avoid here consideration of operations in space, in which all services have a potential interest.) In the case of the Army, the land environment would be defined as including the land itself and the contiguous layers of air and sea necessary for use in ground operations. An analogous definition of air and naval environments would apply for the Air Force and Navy. Fundamental to this functional delineation of the military services would be the right of each service to possess all the weapons and equipment habitually needed in the execution of its functions. Thus, more than one service might properly possess the same weapons, provided they were shown to be habitually necessary for combat in its particular medium.

In November, 1956, at the time of the decision on the operational employment of the IRBM, I urged Secretary Wilson to adopt what I call the National Arsenal concept with regard to the new missiles. Under this concept, any service would be allowed to develop and eventually to produce any missile which the Department of Defense determined to be needed in the national defense and technically within its competence to produce. Once the missile was in existence, it would be regarded as belonging to a National Arsenal from which it could be withdrawn and used by any service needing it in the discharge of its approved missions. I would now propose to revive this National Arsenal concept and make it applicable to all weapons and all the equipment needed by the services to perform their approved functions in their assigned environment.

This proposed revision of service roles and missions would affect primarily the Army and the Air Force and would have little bearing upon the Navy. The Navy is presently organized and equipped for sustained combat in a naval environment. During all the debates on unification in 1946 and '47, the Navy successfully fought for the concept of balanced, self-contained naval forces, including sea, air, and land components. Thus, during the ensuing years, the Navy has been a satisfied service and a stanch defender of the *status quo* in interservice relationships. Navy leaders have viewed with some amusement, I am sure, the unhappiness of the Army in its relations to the Air Force, and have tended to say "I told you so" to the Army chiefs who struggled so hard for unification to the ultimate detriment of their role in sustained ground combat.

The effect of the redefinition of the services would be fundamental in the case of the Army and the Air Force. Since 1947, the Army has been dependent upon the Air Force for tactical air support, tactical air lift, and for long-range air transport. Throughout this period, the Army has been a dissatisfied customer, feeling that the Air Force has not fully discharged its obligations undertaken at the time of unification. The Air Force, having something which the Army wanted, has been in a position to put a price upon co-operation and to insist upon acquiescence in Air Force views on such controversial issues as air-ground support procedures, air resupply, and control of air space over the battlefield. As technical improvements in weapons and equipment offered the Army the possibility of escaping from dependence upon the Air Force, the latter has vigorously resisted these efforts and has succeeded in obtaining the support of the Secretary of Defense in imposing limitations on the size and weight of aircraft procured by the Army, on the ranges of Army missiles, and on the radius of Army activities in advance of the front line of combat.

As a result of the controversies arising from the dependence of the Army on the Air Force, the two services have been constantly at loggerheads. They have been unable to agree on a doctrine for co-operation in battle. They are at odds as to the adequacy of levels of Air Force support for the Army, and as to the suitability of types of Air Force equipment to furnish this support. Because of the very high performance of their airplanes, designed primarily to meet the needs of the air battle today, the Air Force is not equipped to discharge its responsibilities to the Army in ground combat. Having witnessed this unhappy state of affairs for over a decade, I am convinced that the Army must be freed from this tutelage and receive all the organic means habitually necessary for prompt and sustained combat on the ground. It should have its own organic tactical air support and tactical air lift, or rather the new weapons and equipment which will perform the functions presently comprehended under those two headings.

Special restrictions of size, weight, and in the case of weapons, of range should be abolished forever and the Army encouraged to exploit technology to the maximum to improve its weapons and equipment habitually necessary for prompt and sustained ground combat. It is essential to end the present fragmentation of the land force function, particularly at a time when the role of land forces should assume increased importance under the strategy of Flexible Response.

It is not fair to stake out these claims for the Army without seeing what they do to the Air Force. This service I would be initially inclined to define as the one charged with providing military forces necessary for sustained combat operations in an air environment. But a little reflection shows that this is a pretty unsubstantial mission at a time when manned aircraft are disappearing, and with them the kind of sustained air operations which justified the creation of the Air Force as a separate arm of the service. Also, it does not recognize the *de facto* position of the Air Force in the long-range missile field. Hence, I would give the Air Force the additional mission of producing land-based forces for the long-range attack of land targets outside the zone of ground combat.

How would this affect the much disputed use of missiles? The Navy would be unaffected. However, the issue would still exist between the Army and the Air Force since both want to fire missiles from the land against land and air targets. How can their respective spheres be delimited?

I would make mobility and the ability to live and operate with the Army in the field the distinguishing characteristic of all Army equipment, to include combat aircraft and missiles. The Air Force would have the forces and equipment characterized by the need for permanent bases and fixed installations. The Army would be adapted primarily to life and operations on an overseas land mass; the Air Force to life at home and operations conducted intermittently against long-range strategic targets. Specifically, the Army would have mobile, surface-to-surface missiles of all necessary ranges (short of the intercontinental ballistic missiles) and all air-defense missiles needed for the defense of its forces in the field and the land area in which they operate. The Air Force would have the ICBM's and the fixed air-defense missiles for the defense of its own installations and bases. This delineation amounts to giving the Air Force essentially the entire mission of continental air defense.

In their broadest aspect, these proposed changes would make the Army an integrated mobile force for ground combat similar to what the Navy is at sea. Such an Army would take over much of the counterattrition function, which is now split up in many quarters of the defense establishment, to the simplification of our functional budgeting. It would have as its motive force the concept of a hard, mobile striking force ready to move and fight anywhere on the ground.

Similarly, the Air Force would obtain integrated control over all parts of the atomic deterrent force based in the Continental United States, to include the offensive and defensive elements and the early-warning service. This integration would effect a tremendous simplification in research and development, operational control problems, and budgeting. It is hard to estimate how many interservice feuds would be eliminated. True, the basic problems would remain but the responsibility for them would be centralized, to the facilitation of the process of decision-making. The Air Force would have as its motive force—no longer the airman's Wide Blue Yonder—but the prevention of general, atomic war through visible readiness of retaliation and of defense of our homeland against surprise attack.

It occurs to me at this point that I have said nothing specifically about strategic air lift. The Army should, I think, have its own aircraft for internal administrative purposes just as all the other services do today. However, the principle of pooling the common-use strategic air lift in the Military Air Transport Service is sound and should be continued as it is. I would, however, urge again the need for a program to modernize the cargo aircraft in MATS and cut down on the long-range administrative aircraft of the services now withheld from the common pool.

It should be emphasized that the changes proposed for the Army and the Air Force should be phased over a considerable period of time. There would be no point, if it were feasible, for the Army to take over the obsolescent weapons and equipment now available for tactical air support and tactical air lift. Similarly, except for the Jupiter IRBM, there are no currently operational surface-to-surface midrange missiles in the National Arsenal which offer attraction to the Army. There would have to be a gradual phasing into the new roles and missions, worked out under the direction of the Secretary of Defense.

Having clarified and restated the fundamental roles and missions of the services, the Department of Defense should then clear out some of the cobwebs which are fogging the thought processes of our senior leadership. Many of these can be expressed as fallacies which, while they may have appeared to have had some validity in the past, have proved unsound with experience. A major effort of this book has been to expose the Great Fallacy that Massive Retaliation is an all-weather, all-purpose strategy which is adequate to cope with any military challenge. Related thereto is the fallacy that preparation for general war is of supreme importance since limited wars are by nature small wars and can be taken care of in the course of our general-war preparations. This is the dangerous kind of fallacy which can become true if we conduct ourselves in accordance with it. If in accepting this assumption of the intrinsic smallness of limited war we limit our military preparations accordingly, it is obvious that our limited wars will indeed be small since we will not be able to fulfill our multiple defense obligations in big ones. The question remains unanswered, however, as to how we will meet the challenge if our opponent is ready for a larger limited war than we. Presumably we would have to capitulate or wage a general atomic war in which there could be no real victory.

Elsewhere we have commented on the fallacy that we are unable to cope with Communist numbers and hence must depend upon weapons of mass destruction. Vital statistics of the world simply do not prove such an assertion. Our inferiority on the ground is self-imposed.

It is also alleged in the Department of Defense that modern atomic weapons reduce the need for manpower, hence the personnel strength of the military establishment may be safely cut. I know from experience that this statement is a fallacy insofar as it applies to the Army. While the possible use of atomic weapons tends to cause a diminution of military strength in forward combat areas, the complexity of modern weapons requires increased numbers of trained personnel farther to the rear for their maintenance. The dispersion of military installations made necessary by the threat of atomic attack creates new manpower requirements. A consideration of the loss of human life which is possible in atomic warfare would justify an almost unlimited increase in trained manpower for loss replacements. A fair statement would be that the availability of atomic weapons calls for a geographical redistribution of manpower while increasing rather than decreasing the over-all requirement in numbers.

One other fallacy which should be mentioned is one to the effect that a good offensive is the best defensive. This statement is usually used to justify additional funds for the Strategic Air Force at the expense of continental air defense. Yet it flies in the face of a fact which every sportsman knows, namely that a winning team in any game must have a balance of offensive and defensive strength. At the time that this book is being written, the Washington Senators are leading the American League in home runs, yet occupy last place in the league standings. The United States cannot afford to be in even second place in the military league in which we are now playing.

The foregoing examples are illustrative of the fuzzy thinking which needs to be swept out of our planning for national defense. Thereafter there are some major changes to be made within the Department of Defense to facilitate the implementation of the new Military Program. It may seem untimely to make such a proposal, since the Department of Defense was presumably thoroughly overhauled in 1958. The fact is that the changes made then were superficial in character and did not touch the fundamental weaknesses which plague the organization.

In Chapter VI, dealing with the Joint Chiefs of Staff system, the point was made that the Chiefs have the advantages and liabilities of any committee in dealing with the issues before them. They can, and do, engage in useful deliberations on matters of policy when time is not a factor and unanimity is not important. But they are not qualified to cope with operational matters which require an immediate decision without awaiting the outcome of debates characteristic of a council of war.

The most important organizational change which I would propose would be to separate the responsibilities of the Joint Chiefs of Staff which can be dealt with by committee methods from those which require one-man responsibility in order to get acceptable results. Having made this separation,

I would dissolve the JCS as it now exists and replace it by a single Defense Chief of Staff for the one-man functions and by a new advisory body called provisionally the Supreme Military Council. The service Chiefs of Staff would lose their Joint Chief hats and would return to their services to act exclusively as Chiefs of Staff to their respective department Secretaries. The new Defense Chief of Staff would preside over the present Joint Staff (I say the *Joint Staff*, not the Joint Chiefs), assisted by two deputy chiefs of staff of the military services other than his own. He would wear four or five stars and be the senior military officer of the United States Government reporting directly to the Secretary of Defense and to the President. He would be legally and overtly a single Chief of Staff, with public responsibility corresponding to his great authority.

The Supreme Military Council, consisting of three four-star officers of the Army, Navy, and Air Force, would be advisory to the Secretary of Defense, to the President, and to the Congress. They would be either retired officers or officers on their last tour of active military duty and would not be carried on the rolls of any service.

The Supreme Military Council would have no permanent Chairman. Each member would perform the functions of Chairman by monthly rotation. The Council would consider matters referred to it by the Secretary of Defense, by the President, or by the Congress, replying either as a corporate body or as individuals, depending upon the nature of the issue. The Council as a body, or any member of it, could initiate a paper on any appropriate military subject, to include comments upon actions of the Defense Chief of Staff. The Council could call before it any military officer of the government to give information or testimony. It would be assisted by a small secretariat, but would depend for staff support largely on existing agencies.

The point has been made that the Supreme Military Council should legally be made advisory to the Congress. This suggestion is made in recognition of the requirement for Congress to receive responsible military advice. This new status would tend to withdraw the Council from the bosom of the Administration and place it somewhere between the Executive and Legislative branches of the government. While this unusual position may cause a shaking of legal heads, nonetheless, the device offers promising possibilities of meeting a requirement not presently filled by the Joint Chiefs of Staff system.

By sorting out the committee-type and the operational-type functions of the Joint Chiefs of Staff and by fixing clear responsibility for their discharge, it would appear that we would overcome most of the disadvantages noted in the present JCS system. It would be a definite step forward to make recognition of the fact that a committee cannot operate a military headquarters in the ballistic missile age. These changes have the great merit of establishing a system with a reasonable chance of surviving if war comes. The present committee system for the conduct of modern operations would break down within the first few hours or days.

So much for the changes which are necessary within the JCS area of the Department of Defense to facilitate the Military Program of Flexible Response. Other changes would be needed elsewhere to institute functional budget-making and to place the Defense Chief of Staff and the Supreme Military Council in proper relationship to the other elements of the Department of Defense. However, the elaboration of these adjustments is unnecessary within the scope of this book.

There is one other essential precondition to the implementation of the Military Program which must be recognized—the need for a fundamental change in our national attitude toward the requirements of our security. Somehow it must be made clear to our citizens that the nation will face a serious crisis beginning about 1961. For a period of years thereafter, the balance of military strength will tip dangerously in favor of the Communist bloc unless we take drastic action now. Some of the necessary action has been suggested in discussing the "quick fixes" which we should initiate at once. These interim measures should be followed by the accelerated midrange program which has also been discussed.

All these actions will require sacrifice on the part of every one of us if we are to get over this dangerous period without intolerable risk. The simplest form of this sacrifice will be the payment of more taxes to support a larger defense budget. It is difficult to estimate how much money will be required to close the gap of our inferiority at the maximum possible rate, but I would suggest that we are talking in terms of a budget of between $50 to $55 billion a year for the next five years. Once the gap is closed, the subsequent budgets need not be so high. This requirement for a bigger budget will exist regardless of any transitory shift in Soviet attitude and behavior. There is no living with Communism as an inferior.

We will also have to commit more of our ablest sons to the profession of arms in this period. The immediate goal of the Army is 925,000, in comparison to the presently authorized 870,000. Thereafter, this Army strength should be increased to a million men, its strength in 1955. The over-all manpower required by all services will amount to at least 2.6 million. These larger forces must be modernized, with the first priority to the needs of the atomic deterrent forces and the counterattrition forces. The United States cannot ask its sons to prepare themselves for battle with less than the best equipment which science and technology can provide.

All the foregoing actions should be taken to the sure notes of a certain trumpet, giving to friend and foe alike a clear expression of our purpose and of our motives. Our military behavior must be visibly consistent with our conduct in the political, economic, and intellectual fields. Our strategic readjustments should not be mistaken for a new spurt in an armament race with the USSR. Any serious imbalance in military power between East and West is an encouragement to war—if it favors the Communist dictatorship. Actions to correct an imbalance of power and to replace the concept of Massive Retaliation by one of Flexible Response are measures conducive not to war but to world peace. Such are the notes to be sounded by confident leaders who know what they are doing and why. Then we can prepare ourselves calmly to the battle, knowing that if it is properly prepared, the odds are high for peace.

APPENDIX

(An article written by the author in the spring of 1956 for *Foreign Affairs* magazine, but not printed in that magazine for reasons apparent in the comments of State and Defense Department reviewers which are inserted as appropriate.)

Security Through Deterrence

by
General Maxwell D. Taylor
Chief of Staff, United States Army

Defense comment:

"It is the opinion of this office that this article should not be released for publication unless it is revised drastically. Following are some of the reasons why it should not be published as an article or delivered as a speech by the Chief of Staff of the Army.

"1. Much of the general subject matter is highly controversial and is in conflict with the established policies of the Joint Chiefs of Staff and the Secretary of Defense.

"2. It proposes changes in national policy planning which should be presented to, and argued before the Joint Chiefs of Staff, and incorporated in Joint Chiefs of Staff recommendations processed through normal channels.

"3. To have the Chief of Staff of the Army give voice to some of the views expressed in the proposed article could seriously jeopardize our international relations.

"Attached is a memorandum from the Department of State setting forth its objections to, and comments on the proposed article.

"If the same theme and tone are incorporated in the revised draft, it is recommended that it be submitted to the Secretary of the Army for his personal review, and that it also be re-submitted to this office for review."

State comment:

"It is the opinion of the Department of State that this material, when it reaches final form for either magazine or speech use, should be very carefully reviewed. There are certain overtones that make it much more the kind of material to be discussed among military personnel on a confidential basis than used for public purposes."

Throughout the Western World, governments are engaged with very difficult problems relating to national defense. In general, they are seeking to determine the types of forces best adapted to their several needs which at the same time are within their economic means.

These considerations of the requirements of national defense are taking place against a common background. In recent years, advances in military technology have made possible the development and production of weapons of great destructive power. They are, however, very expensive both in their initial cost and in their subsequent maintenance. Furthermore, the destructiveness of some of them limits their application and creates uncertainties as to the conditions of their employment. The situation is made no easier by the fact that the decision to invest heavy sums for their procurement must be taken in a situation of relaxing tensions amid renewed discussions of possible disarmament. Under such conditions, it is not surprising that most governments are reluctant to obtain these new weapons by direct increases to their already high military budgets. Instead, they are either delaying the procurement of the new weapons, or are seeking to offset their acquisition costs by personnel reductions.

A further difficulty in deciding upon weapons and defense force structures is the uncertainty as to the form which future war will take. Will it be general or local? Will atomic weapons be used without restriction, under certain ground rules, or not at all? Will the homelands of the opposing national blocs be primary atomic targets, or will relative equality in destructive power on both sides result in a situation of mutual deterrence insofar as such attacks are concerned? Is it possible to limit atomic weapons to battlefield use without bringing on general atomic war? The difficulty of obtaining categorical answers to questions such as these complicates the work of those who must plan military programs and explains in part the lack of unanimity in their views.

The planners are further impeded in developing properly balanced programs by the surcharged emotions arising from fear of the great atomic war. So much has been written about the dreadfulness of atomic warfare that a dispassionate analysis of the requirements of national defense is made difficult by a fixation on the overriding importance of the one Big War. This fixation, sometimes called the One War Concept, leads to a feeling that all efforts should be directed toward preparing for a general atomic war. It is usually accompanied by an attitude of indifference or disregard toward the possibility of lesser forms of aggression, although the latter may ultimately prove as disadvantageous to our nation as the Big War and, indeed, may induce it. This blurred perception of where the real dangers lie is particularly apparent in the United States, which for the first time finds itself a possible target for direct enemy attack.

This paper undertakes to discuss the development of a national military program, based upon the philosophy of deterrence, which will try to avoid the dangers arising from concentration of effort on any one preconceived form of warfare. It is directed at the military needs of the United States but has some application to those of our allies. It takes as its point of departure the premise that the purpose of a proper national military program is to deter war, particularly the general atomic war which will be so mutually destructive as to offer little choice between the fruits of victory or defeat. So compelling is the need to prevent this kind of war that it follows as corollary that the requirements of its deterrence should be amply met before other steps are taken to hedge against the failure of deterrence and to make additional preparations for fighting a general nuclear war.

The avoidance of deliberate general atomic war should not be too difficult since its unremunerative character must be clear to the potential adversaries. Although actual stockpile sizes are closely guarded secrets, a nation need only feel reasonably sure that an opponent has some high-yield weapons, no matter how indefinite their exact number, to be impressed with the possible consequences of attacking him. [*State comment: "The paragraph . . . concerning the question of the avoidance*

of general atomic war, especially the opening sentence, is considered unfortunate. The casual way this vital matter is brought in, and the vast understatement and simplification implied in the first two sentences merit very careful review."]
It is true that there is always the possibility of "backing into" the Big War, either by mistake or by way of a series of smaller military undertakings which expand into general war. With the past record of the Communist bloc for infiltration, subversion, and local aggression, this latter possibility seems to require particular consideration. In view of the rather encouraging success of its past efforts, there is no reason to believe that Communism will change its future habits and permanently renounce aggression as an instrument of policy. [*State comment: "This sentence . . . contains two factors which we would prefer not stressed. One is any mention of the 'rather encouraging success' of Soviet efforts, since the United States line has been that their aggressive methods have been at least temporarily abandoned because of their failure. The second point is that it is generally recognized that the Communists for the present have renounced aggression as an instrument of policy, and, therefore, part of this sentence is not only undesirable but inaccurate."*] In a period when the atomic air fleets of the opposing power blocs offset one another by their countervailing threats, it would seem increasingly likely that the dynamism of Communism will become more likely than ever to seek an outlet in the form of aggression with limited objectives. If such pressures are unresisted, the Free World will be exposed to loss through piecemeal erosion; if resisted, there will be the danger of general war developing out of a local "brush fire."

If the foregoing reasoning is correct, in addition to the objective of deterring the Big War, an adequate military program must provide means of deterring limited aggression, or of quickly suppressing it before it can grow. Not only is rapid reaction necessary to prevent piecemeal losses, but to limit the danger that the small war, if allowed to drag out, will grow into the Big War which it is our purpose to avoid. Thus, a national military program must make early and adequate provision for responding effectively to local aggression wherever it occurs.

In passing, it is of some interest to reflect upon the effect of mutual deterrence—i.e., rough equivalence on both sides in air-atomic retaliatory power—upon the possible size of military operations short of general war. It seems reasonable to assume that, in a situation where both sides are capable of inflicting crippling damage on the other in unrestricted nuclear warfare, each side will tend to accept an increasingly high level of provocation before deliberately resorting to general atomic warfare. Indeed, it seems fair to assume that if the two blocs are governed by rational men, they will initiate general atomic warfare only as a last desperate act *in extremis*. [*State comment: "It is questioned whether this sentence . . . should usefully be said in public. We have never implied in any way that we will 'initiate' atomic warfare but only retaliate, yet the implication is very obvious here that we are part of one of the two 'blocs' to which the statement refers."*] Under such conditions, it may be anticipated that military operations of considerable size may take place without expansion to general war, since it would be a matter of mutual interest to keep the hostilities localized. For similar reasons, it also seems likely that there will be a desire to limit, if not to prevent, the use of atomic weapons in local conflicts for fear of their unpredictable consequences in broadening the war. These tendencies to restrict atomic weapons may also find support from the proprietor of the battle zone, presumably a friend to whom we are bringing military aid to resist aggression. There is such destructiveness in atomic weapons, even in the small ones, that serious objection to their use in friendly territory may be anticipated from the inhabitants.

These preliminary remarks have outlined the so-called philosophy of deterrence and some of its related aspects. It is now time to attempt to develop the specific elements of a national military program which will emphasize deterrence and concentrate its efforts on the prevention of general atomic war. Specifically, what are the weapons and types of forces which should receive priority allocation of means in consistence with the deterrent approach outlined above?

It is felt that the following represent the essential elements of a national military program designed, in order of priority: to deter general war, to deter or win local war, and finally, to cope with a general war if deterrence fails. These elements are listed in order of general priority, but this priority cannot be preclusive. In other words, the list shows the order of emphasis, but we must provide in some degree for all components of the program outlined.

At the top of such a priority list is placed the maintenance of military technological superiority over the Communist bloc. We cannot long remain secure if we do not have the potentiality of outstripping an enemy in the quality of our weapons systems. The missile program springs readily to mind as typical of the exploitation of technology to extend the tactical and strategical capabilities of our armed forces. Our country can never afford to relax its efforts in this technological field, feeling sure that our potential adversaries are doing their best to equal or outstrip us.

Immediately after technological progress, there should be general agreement to making adequate provision for an atomic delivery system capable of effective and rapid retaliation against any enemy who initiates atomic hostilities against us. At the present time this atomic delivery capability resides primarily in the long- and medium-range bombers of the Air Force and of the Navy; but it will be reinforced in the course of coming years by other weapons systems, notably the long- and medium-range missiles now under design and development.

The deterrent effectiveness of this retaliatory atomic force depends on two essential factors. The first is the obvious ability of the force to do its job of retaliatory destruction, an ability which depends not merely on numbers of airplanes but on their quality and their protection from surprise attack. Because of the destructive power of modern atomic weapons, the number of aircraft and missiles required to wreak catastrophic damage is not particularly great. It is most important, however, that they be of the highest technical quality so that there can be no doubt about their ability to penetrate to the target; furthermore, that they be dispersed and protected on their departure bases so that an aggressor seeking the advantage of surprise cannot count upon the destruction of a significant part of the retaliatory force.

There is also an important psychological factor which must be present to make this retaliatory weapon effective. It must be clear to the aggressor that we have the will and determination to use our retaliatory power without compunction if we are attacked. Any suggestion of weakness or indecision may encourage the enemy to gamble on surprise.

Along with the visible ability to strike hard and decisively in retaliation against the sources of enemy war-making strength, there should be an equally unmistakable capacity to inflict heavy loss on enemy bombers if they attack our homeland. This requirement calls for a continental defense system, including both active and passive measures strong enough to discourage any enemy from attempting to strike with surprise a crippling blow at our atomic delivery system or at the war-making resources of our country. For the time being, the Army's antiaircraft missiles and the Air Force's fighter interceptors represent the essential elements of this defensive system. Continental air defense is an area in which it is difficult to know how much is enough in meeting the needs of deterrence. It is easy to go overboard in spending for continental air defense to the detriment of other important offensive aspects of our military program. Continental air defense is essential national damage insurance, but it would be a mistake to attempt to try to achieve 100 per cent coverage to protect against all risks. Such a coverage cannot be obtained without loss of balance in the over-all military program.

Another indispensable element of our deterrent system consists of our military forces deployed abroad, ready for sustained combat in the discharge of our international obligations. These forces, deployed to cover vital strategic areas in Europe and in the Far East, are a constant reminder of our determination to defend in place. Our present forces in these areas are large enough to provide a significant military contribution which, in conjunction with the indigenous forces of our allies, are capable of sustained resistance if attacked.

We have spoken of the dangers of surprise air attack against our homeland. A similar danger exists for our forces overseas. In Europe, we have some 250,000 soldiers accompanied by thousands of dependents living in close proximity to superior Communist ground forces deployed in the satellite countries. If the latter suddenly advanced west without warning, they would soon be locked in close combat with the NATO armies in such a way as to restrict the employment of atomic weapons against them. [*State comment: ". . . it is seriously questioned whether the statement about the restrictions to the use of atomic weapons in relation to the NATO armies should be stated in public."*] Thus, it is most important to have strong, alert ground forces in Europe capable of discouraging any such surprise attack or of holding it at a distance long enough to permit the unhampered use of our retaliatory weapons.

It is worth emphasizing that to cope with this danger of surprise ground attack, token Army forces are not sufficient. There must be real strength on the ground to provide the necessary buffer capable of holding back the attacker. There is talk in Europe of "trip-wire" ground forces as sufficient to provide this protection and to trigger the release of atomic destruction upon aggressor ground forces. While this trip-wire concept may offer some relief to military budgets, it provides no assurance of producing an adequate deterrent effect upon the enemy. There must be real defensive strength in being to gain adequate reaction time for the counterblows necessary to destroy the invader. Also, the trip-wire solution to ground forces assumes a willingness in the West to incur in a period of mutual deterrence the risks of general atomic war for the sake of such forces.

If these overseas deployments are to effect maximum deterrence, it should be possible to reinforce them and to sustain them in combat. Thus, our program must provide for mobile, ready forces prepared for rapid movement to areas of strategic importance overseas. These forces will back up not only our overseas forces but also the initial expeditionary force for use to resist local aggression in an unexpected quarter. These forces should be equipped with both atomic and conventional weapons in order to be able to adapt themselves to any decision bearing on the use of atomic weapons. They will look to the Air Force and the Navy to provide the most expeditious form of transport. By advance planning to include the forward positioning of heavy equipment, the tonnage to be lifted and hence the time lag of reaction may be substantially reduced.

The need to support our overseas deployments and to meet local aggression promptly is but one of the many reasons why the national military program must make adequate provision for naval surface forces, apart from the naval air component participating in the air retaliatory force. The Navy is needed to keep the essential sea lanes open, particularly those communicating with possible overseas theaters of war. The rate and weight of the United States military reaction to aggression will depend upon the uninterrupted use of sea communications. The task of assuring this freedom of movement becomes increasingly difficult for our Navy as modern submarines improve in design. Hence, the national military program should provide a strong antisubmarine warfare component for the Navy.

Because of the importance of having allies with adequate

military forces, particularly ground forces, we should include at this point in our priority list an appropriate item for aid to allies. This aid should be related to the military contribution which we desire from the recipient countries. Generally speaking, we hope for one of three levels of military strength in these countries. As a minimum, we want all to have the necessary military strength to assure internal stability and order. Beyond this minimum level, we wish in some instances to develop a capability for self-defense against local military aggression. Finally, in a rather restricted group of countries we seek to develop allies who can make a significant and prolonged contribution in case of general war. [*State comment:* "... *the sentence beginning 'Finally, in a rather restricted group of countries ...'—It is believed that our motivation for the development of alliances has been vastly simplified. The contribution of this group of allies in case of general war is only one factor here, and certainly not a motive that we should attribute publicly as the sole one."*] In the ideal case, the combination of local military resources with the contribution which the United States might make should provide the strength required to support our strategic objectives in the area.

Thus far, the priority elements of our military program have been assets in being: technological superiority, an atomic retaliatory force, a continental air defense, overseas deployments, naval forces to maintain sea communications, and indigenous forces supported in varying degrees by our military aid. In the aggregate, they will have very considerable strength and should present a persuasive argument to an enemy for the maintenance of peace. However, it would be imprudent if we failed to make some provision for back-up strength capable of reinforcing our active forces in a period of tension prior to hostilities or after hostilities have begun.

One hears doubts expressed about the possibility of a so-called conventional mobilization in case of future war. Generally, these doubts are based on the assumption that the war under consideration is a general atomic war, initiated by a surprise onslaught against our homeland. In such an event, it is indeed doubtful that any mobilization resembling that of World War II could take place. However, even in a general atomic war the degree of destruction which might be effected by the enemy is impossible to forecast. Fortunately, it is by no means certain or even likely that a future war will start with a D-Day atomic onslaught. It may well be to the self-interest of both parties to refrain from the unrestricted use of atomic weapons for reasons advanced in the previous discussions. [*State comment: "It is believed that the last sentence . . . should be deleted. Surely the strength of our deterrent position is that we will use the ultimate weapon against all-out aggression."*]

The requirements for mobilization are, of course, relative to the size of a war and the circumstances under which it is fought. The Korean War, although local in size and limited in objective, required very extensive mobilization activities in order to support it. Any distant military operation will always be difficult and expensive, causing a serious drain on our national resources. As previously mentioned, in a period of mutual deterrence the size and extent of military operations short of general war seem likely to increase as the reluctance to accept the dangers of general war increases. Consequently, it appears imperative to make some provision in our plans for reserve forces, supplies, and equipment. It is doubtful, however, when we get down to specific costs that we can make anything like the provision for these items which the logisticians, habitually a conservative group, are likely to recommend.

At this point, we might draw a line and total up the price of the foregoing military program in terms of men, money, and materials. There should be no illusion that we have designed a cheap or easy military program. Exactly how much it will cost will require additional painstaking work on the part of the military planners who will be faced with determining what constitutes adequacy in the various elements of the program. Without making a specific estimate, one may be sure that the total bill will exceed any peacetime budget in United States history. On the other hand, the money will have been allocated very largely to buy deterrent strength. Without giving absolute protection, the program will offer a strong probability of being able to deter war, both general and local, and to win local war quickly. At the same time, by dispersion and continental air defense measures, it will have made prudent provision to protect our retaliatory and war-making potential from destruction by surprise attack.

At least one serious criticism may be leveled at this program. It is predicated upon faith in the effectiveness of deterrence and makes incomplete provision for the fact that deterrence may fail and that the United States may undergo a destructive atomic attack. It is true that the foregoing program does not provide for anything like all of the requirements which might ensue from such an attack. These requirements in full are beyond our national means. If we accept the assumption that heavy atomic bomb damage is so probable that our country must make advance provision for it, there is no end to the military and civil defense requirements thus generated. In all logic we should create larger military forces in being to compensate for those probably to be lost through bomb attack. Stockpiles of supplies should be made larger in order to offset the anticipated losses. Heavy additional expenditures could be justified for air warning systems, to thicken the air defenses of vital areas, and to improve civil defense measures. Every city, town, and hamlet should make preparations on the assumption that it will be attacked; indeed, to be consistent with our fears, we should disperse our principal centers of population and remake our entire economy.

The requirements for survival in general war could be used as a reason not only to remake our life at home but also to revamp our foreign policy and to modify our military commitments to allies. If we assume that general atomic war is the only war worth preparing for and that such a war will begin with a crippling atomic attack on the United States, it follows that we will not be able to support in combat our forces abroad or to send help to our allies. Hence we should bring our forces home before it is too late and adjust our commitments to our allies in the light of our reduced capability to help. Such action, however, would alienate those allies, increase their reluctance to allow us the use of their territory for forward bases, and encourage trends toward neutralization. From thence, it is a short step for us to the abandonment of our present forward strategy based on the NATO alliance and to the search for security in entrenched isolation. [*State comment: "Attention was particularly invited to this paragraph. . . . The opinion here is that this kind of speculation is not for public discussion, and it is recommended that the paragraph in its entirety be deleted. This would mean that the following paragraph should be considerably revised to play down the implication that 'lack of faith in deterrence' figures very definitely in the national policy at the present time."*]

Faced with the decisions which would flow from a lack of faith in deterrence and from a fixation on the requirements of survival in general atomic war, our national planners will, it is hoped, choose to support the flexible program of deterrence outlined above. If so, they will insist upon first making adequate provision for those forces which clearly contribute to deterrence, allocating only whatever can be afforded thereafter for hedging against the failure of deterrence. Thus, we will live with some risk, but in a way which seems preferable to a dreary existence in caves and deserts, the prospect offered if we act consistently with the assumption that the only war worth preparing for is surprise, nuclear attack on the United States.

In contrast, the military program of deterrence recommended herein has flexibility to cope with various forms of military action. It is geared to no one weapons system, to no fixed concept of future war. It is not blind to the awful dangers of general atomic war; indeed, it takes as its primary purpose the avoidance of that catastrophe. At the same time, it makes due recognition of the need to cope with situations short of general war. It undertakes to maintain a forward posture designed to keep war as far as possible from our shores. It should reassure rather than repel allies. Most important, it will permit our national leaders a wide range of choice when at some future critical moment of history they must determine the appropriate military reaction required by our national interest. [*State comment: "The final consideration of the article—the need for flexibility—is perfectly acceptable, of course, but the strong thread that runs through the entire 13 pages—that the policy of deterrence is in grave question— should be watered down and made much more speculative."*]

INDEX

Adenauer, Konrad, 42
Africa, Communists in, 60
Air defense, 97-98, 155-156, 161, 171, *see also* Strategic Air Command (SAC)
Air Force, *see* United States Air Force
Air lift, strategic, 172
Air power, 11-18, 51
Aircraft, manned, 98, 99, 133-134, 170
Aircraft carriers, 101-102
Anderson, Robert B., 70, 71
Antisubmarine warfare, 53, 100, 102, 157-158, 160, 161
Appropriations Committees, 111
Armed Forces Policy Council, 49
Armed Services Committees, 111
Armstrong, Hamilton Fish, 43
Army, *see* United States Army
Atlas missile, 67
Atomic fall-out, *see* Fall-out
Atomic weapons, 1, 3-4, 12-13, 25-26, 38-39, 45, 46, 56, 59, 117, 174

B-36 program, 14
Baghdad Pact, 60
"Basic National Security Policy," 22, 60, 61, 64, 65, 78, 81-83, 84, 85, 91, 95, 115, 116
"Basic National Security Policy" (1955), 26-27, 29
"Basic National Security Policy" (1958), 57
Berchtesgaden, 1-2
Berlin, 6, 8, 13, 136, 154
Bomarc missile, 67, 98, 119, 120
Bradley, General Omar, 18, 20, 110
Braun, Dr. Wernher von, 140
Brodie, Bernard, 26
Brucker, Wilber M., 30, 49, 50, 52
Budget, *see* Defense budget
Bureau of the Budget, 52, 54, 80, 122, 163
Burke, Arleigh, 73
Bush, Vannevar, 26

Carney, Admiral Robert, 18
Chairman, JCS, 106-111
"Challenge and Response in United States Policy," 55-56
China, 45, 138
Coffman, W. W., 26
Collins, General J. Lawton, 19
Communists, 31-34, 45, 60, 145, 153,

154, 173, 178, *see also* China; Russia

Council on Foreign Relations, 43

Czechoslovakia, 13

Decision-making, 115-129

Defense budget, 21, 25, 37-38, 46, 47-49, 51-54, 92, 105, 111, 121-124, 127-128, 158, 178-179, *also passim*

Defense budget (1960), 65-70, 72-78, 92, 127

Defense budget (1961), 78

Defense budget ceilings, 52, 87

Defense Chief of Staff, proposed, 176-177

Department of Defense, *see* United States Department of Defense

Dien Bien Phu, 24-25

Douhet, General Giulio, 11-12

Dulles, John Foster, 55-57, 65

Early-warning program, 67, 159

Earth satellites, 48, 53, 63

Eisenhower, Dwight D., 17, 18, 29, 71, 121, 123

Eisenhower Administration, 17-18

Eniwetok, 1952 bomb test, 25

Fall-out, 133, 139, 140, 157, 158

Fall-out shelters, *see* Shelters

Fechteler, Admiral William M., 18

Flexible Response Strategy, 6-7, 30, 36, 83, 95, 97, 98, 100, 108, 116, 130-164, 165, 170, 178, 179, *see also* Limited wars; Massive Retaliation concept

Foreign Affairs, 43, 55, 181

Formosa, 45, 136

"Fortress America" concept, 41, 98, 101

France, Indochina loss, 24-25

"General war," definition of, 7, 8, 39

Gray, Gordon, 70

Greece, 1947 Civil War, 9, 13

Groves, General Leslie R., Jr., 3

Guderian, General, 2

Hart, B. H. Liddell, 26

Heusinger, General Adolf, 42

Hiroshima, 12

Holloway, Admiral James, 92-93

Hull, General John E., 27

Hungary, 47, 48

Hydrogen bombs, 25, 99

ICBM's, 171

IRBM program, 67, 139-142, 167, 172

"Indians," 90

Indochina, 24-25

Indonesia, 60

Interservice rivalry, 105

JCS, *see* Joint Chiefs of Staff

Johnson, Senator Lyndon B., 73

Joint Chiefs of Staff, 18-22, 36-43, 45, 46, 48, 49, 53, 54, 55, 57, 61, 69, 84-85, 87, 175

Chairman, 106-111

and Congress, 111-114

decision-making, 115-129

"Indians," 90

"JCS Position on the FY 1960 Budget," 74

Operational Deputies, 88

and Secretary of Defense, 109-110

split paper, 106

work procedure, 88-114

Joint Staff, proposed, 176

"Joint Strategic Objectives Plan" (JSOP), 22, 38, 85-87

Jupiter missile, 67, 140-142, 172

Kennan, George F., 26
Kesselring, Field Marshal, 2
Key West Agreement, 165
Key West conference (1947), 165
Korean War, 5, 9, 14-18, 21, 23-25, 27, 45, 77, 137, 154, 157

Laos, 6, 136
Lebanon, 9-10, 92-93, 151, 153
Leviero, Anthony, 41
Limited war, concept and problems, 58, 98-99, 103, 108, 117, 135, 145-146, 149-151, 153, 159, 173, *see also* Flexible Response Strategy
"Limited war," definition of, 7-9, 59, 62-63
Limited War Headquarters, proposed, 143-144

McElroy, Neil, 65, 69-70, 72, 92, 120, 123
Malaya, 45
Manpower, 138, 179
Manpower in Fit Males (table), 138
Marine Corps, *see* United States Marine Corps
Marshall, General George C., 1, 2-4, 90
Marshall aid, 154
Massive Retaliation concept, 4-5, 10, 11-18, 26-30, 36, 39, 43, 46, 48, 49, 55-58, 59-62, 78, 83, 95, 100-103, 110, 116, 128, 136, 146, 173, 179, *see also* Flexible Response Strategy; Limited war
Medaris, General John B., 140
Middle East, 47, 60, 95, 136
Military Air Transport Service (MATS), 172

Military strategy, *see* United States military strategy
Missile Gap concept, 131
Missiles and missile programs, 53, 58, 67-68, 75, 76, 77-78, 91, 97-98, 99, 100, 103, 104, 105, 130-134, 136, 139, 140-142, 148-149, 155, 159, 161, 167, 169, 170, 171, 172, *see also particular names*, e.g., Jupiter; Nike-Zeus; etc.

NATO, 9, 57, 60, 61, 62, 137, 145
Nagasaki, 12
National Arsenal concept, 167, 172
"National Military Program," of Army, 29-35, 43
"National Military Program," of Defense Department, 115
National Security Council (NSC), 21-22, 26-27, 29-30, 47-52, 54, 59-60, 72, 80-83, 84, 85, 87, 95, 115, 116, 146
Navy, *see* United States Navy
"New Look" program, 5, 17-22, 23-79, 110, 121, 137
New Look (1953-1956), 23-46
New Look (1956-1959), 47-79
New York Times, 41
Nike-Ajax missiles, 67
Nike-Hercules missiles, 67
Nike-Zeus missiles, 67-69, 75, 76, 98, 101, 104, 119, 120, 131-132, 149, 159, 161
Nixon, Richard, 70
Norstad, General Lauris, 92-93
North Africa, 60
North Vietnam, 45
Nuclear-powered submarines, 58
Nuclear weapons, *see* Atomic weapons

Index

101st Airborne Division, 1
Operational Deputies, 88

"Parable of the Unhappy Mess Sergeant," 124-127
Pate, R. McC., 73
Patton, General George S., 1, 2-3, 4
Polaris missile, 67, 100, 104, 105, 134, 149
Priorities, table of, 159-162
Puerto Rico, 1956 JCS meeting, 36-38, 120

Quarles, Donald A., 49, 118, 121
"Quick fixes," 139-144, 152

Radford, Admiral Arthur, 18, 38-42, 44, 48, 49, 52, 106, 107, 108, 110, 118, 121
Ramey Air Force Base, Puerto Rico, 1956 Joint Chiefs of Staff meeting, 36-38
Randall, General Carey, 49, 50
Realities of American Foreign Policy, The, 26
Ridgway, General Matthew B., 15, 19, 23, 24, 27, 28, 29, 108
Rivalry, between services, 105
Russia, 6, 7, 8, 13, 16, 25, 26, 31-34, 38-39, 41, 45, 48-50, 53, 55, 59, 60, 61, 63, 64, 68, 102-103, 117, 130-136, 137-139, 142, 145, 148, 154, 155, 157, 158, 159, 160, 179

SEATO, 60
Satellites, man-made, 48, 53, 63
Secretary of Defense, 115, 120-121, 162-163, 169
Secretary of Defense, and JCS Chairman, 109-110
"Security Through Deterrence," 43-44, 181-197

Senate, see United States Senate
Service rivalry, 105
Shelters, 139, 140, 157
Skifter, Hector R., 69
Soviet Union, see Russia
Sputnik I, 48, 53, 63
Stans, Maurice H., 70
Stevens, Robert, 27, 28
Strategic Air Command (SAC), 53, 94, 101, 103, 104, 143, 174
Submarines, nuclear-powered, 58, 158
Suez, 47, 48
Supreme Military Council, proposed, 176-177

Taft, Robert A., 20
Taiwan, see Formosa
Taxes, for defense budget, 178
Taylor, Maxwell D., 73, 181
Taylor, Mrs. Maxwell D., 28
Thor missile, 67, 142
Titan missile, 67
Truman Administration, 13, 17, 19, 20
Twining, General Nathan F., 19, 64, 72, 73, 107, 110, 121

U. S. Strategic Bombing Survey, 12
USSR, see Russia
United States:
    Air Force, 11, 13-14, 58-59, 64, 66, 67, 68, 141, 166-167, 168-172
    Air Force position on national strategy, 102-105
    Army, 13-14, 37, 39-40, 47, 49, 50, 51, 52, 53-54, 57-58, 66, 67, 166-167, 168-172, 179
    Army position on national strategy, 97-99

United States—*Continued*
Congress, relations with JCS, 111-114
Department of Defense, 106, 111, 115, 118, 165, 166, 175, *also passim*
Department of Defense Reorganization Act (1958), 106, 166, 175
Marine Corps, 58, 66, 100-102
military strategy, fact, 115-129
military strategy, theory, 80-87
Navy, 14, 58, 66, 67, 101-102, 166-167, 168
Navy-Marine Corps, position on national strategy, 100-102

United States—*Continued*
Senate Preparedness Investigating Committee, 73-75

V-E Day, 1
Vandenberg, General Hoyt S., 19

Weapons, atomic, *see* Atomic weapons
Weapons, new, 119-120
Weible, General Walter, 28
White, General Thomas W., 64, 73
Wilson, Charles, 28-29, 37-38, 42, 48-49, 50, 51, 52, 118, 120, 123, 140-141

Set in Janson
Format by Seamus Byrne
Manufactured by The Haddon Craftsmen, Inc.
Published by HARPER & BROTHERS, *New York*